TOUCHSTONE

SECOND EDITION

STUDENT'S BOOK 3B

MICHAEL McCARTHY

JEANNE McCARTEN

HELEN SANDIFORD

CAMBRIDGE
UNIVERSITY PRESS

CAMBRIDGE
UNIVERSITY PRESS

University Printing House, Cambridge CB2 8BS, United Kingdom

One Liberty Plaza, 20th Floor, New York, NY 10006, USA

477 Williamstown Road, Port Melbourne, VIC 3207, Australia

314–321, 3rd Floor, Plot 3, Splendor Forum, Jasola District Centre, New Delhi – 110025, India

103 Penang Road, #05-06/07, Visioncrest Commercial, Singapore 238467

Cambridge University Press is part of the University of Cambridge.

It furthers the University's mission by disseminating knowledge in the pursuit of education, learning and research at the highest international levels of excellence.

www.cambridge.org
Information on this title: www.cambridge.org/9781107694460

First published 2005
Second Edition 2014

20 19 18 17

Printed in Great Britain by CPI Group (UK) Ltd, Croydon CR0 4YY

A catalogue record for this publication is available from the British Library

ISBN 978-1-107-66583-5 Student's Book
ISBN 978-1-107-62875-5 Student's Book A
ISBN 978-1-107-69446-0 Student's Book B
ISBN 978-1-107-64271-3 Workbook
ISBN 978-1-107-62082-7 Workbook A
ISBN 978-1-107-65147-0 Workbook B
ISBN 978-1-107-62794-9 Full Contact
ISBN 978-1-107-63739-9 Full Contact A
ISBN 978-1-107-63903-4 Full Contact B
ISBN 978-1-107-68094-4 Teacher's Edition with Assessment Audio CD/CD-ROM
ISBN 978-1-107-63179-3 Class Audio CDs (4)

Additional resources for this publication at www.cambridge.org/touchstone2

Acknowledgments

Touchstone Second Edition has benefited from extensive development research. The authors and publishers would like to extend their thanks to the following reviewers and consultants for their valuable insights and suggestions:

Ana Lúcia da Costa Maia de Almeida and Mônica da Costa Monteiro de Souza from **IBEU**, Rio de Janeiro, Brazil; Andreza Cristiane Melo do Lago from **Magic English School**, Manaus, Brazil; Magaly Mendes Lemos from **ICBEU**, São José dos Campos, Brazil; Maria Lucia Zaorob, São Paulo, Brazil; Patricia McKay Aronis from **CEL LEP**, São Paulo, Brazil; Carlos Gontow, São Paulo, Brazil; Christiane Augusto Gomes da Silva from **Colégio Visconde de Porto Seguro**, São Paulo, Brazil; Silvana Fontana from **Lord's Idiomas**, São Paulo, Brazil; Alexander Fabiano Morishigue from **Speed Up Idiomas**, Jales, Brazil; Elisabeth Blom from **Casa Thomas Jefferson**, Brasília, Brazil; Michelle Dear from **International Academy of English**, Toronto, ON, Canada; Walter Duarte Marin, Laura Hurtado Portela, Jorge Quiroga, and Ricardo Suarez, from **Centro Colombo Americano**, Bogotá, Colombia; Jhon Jairo Castaneda Macias from **Praxis English Academy**, Bucaramanga, Colombia; Gloria Liliana Moreno Vizcaino from **Universidad Santo Tomas**, Bogotá, Colombia; Elizabeth Ortiz from **Copol English Institute (COPEI)**, Guayaquil, Ecuador; Henry Foster from **Kyoto Tachibana University**, Kyoto, Japan; Steven Kirk from **Tokyo University**, Tokyo, Japan; J. Lake from **Fukuoka Woman's University**, Fukuoka, Japan; Etsuko Yoshida from **Mie University**, Mie, Japan; B. Bricklin Zeff from **Hokkai Gakuen University**, Hokkaido, Japan; Ziad Abu-Hamatteh from **Al-Balqa' Applied University**, Al-Salt, Jordan; Roxana Pérez Flores from **Universidad Autonoma de Coahuila Language Center**, Saltillo, Mexico; Kim Alejandro Soriano Jimenez from **Universidad Politecnica de Altamira**, Altamira, Mexico; Tere Calderon Rosas from **Universidad Autonoma Metropolitana Campus Iztapalapa**, Mexico City, Mexico; Lilia Bondareva, Polina Ermakova, and Elena Frumina, from **National Research Technical University MISiS**, Moscow, Russia; Dianne C. Ellis from **Kyung Hee University**, Gyeonggi-do, South Korea; Jason M. Ham and Victoria Jo from **Institute of Foreign Language Education, Catholic University of Korea**, Gyeonggi-do, South Korea; Shaun Manning from **Hankuk University of Foreign Studies**, Seoul, South Korea; Natalie Renton from **Busan National University of Education**, Busan, South Korea; Chris Soutter from **Busan University of Foreign Studies**, Busan, South Korea; Andrew Cook from **Dong A University**, Busan, South Korea; Raymond Wowk from **Daejin University**, Gyeonggi-do, South Korea; Ming-Hui Hsieh and Jessie Huang from **National Central University**, Zhongli, Taiwan; Kim Phillips from **Chinese Culture University**, Taipei, Taiwan; Alex Shih from **China University of Technology**, Taipei Ta-Liao Township, Taiwan; Porntip Bodeepongse from **Thaksin University**, Songkhla, Thailand; Nattaya Puakpong and Pannathon Sangarun from **Suranaree University of Technology**, Nakhon Ratchasima, Thailand; Barbara Richards, Gloria Stewner-Manzanares, and Caroline Thompson, from **Montgomery College**, Rockville, MD, USA; Kerry Vrabel from **Gateway Community College**, Phoenix, AZ, USA.

Touchstone Second Edition authors and publishers would also like to thank the following individuals and institutions who have provided excellent feedback and support on *Touchstone Blended*:

Gordon Lewis, Vice President, Laureate Languages and Chris Johnson, Director, Laureate English Programs, Latin America from **Laureate International Universities**; **Universidad de las Americas**, Santiago, Chile; **University of Victoria**, Paris, France; **Universidad Technólogica Centroamericana**, Honduras; **Institut Universitaire de Casablanca**, Morocco; **Universidad Peruana de Ciencias Aplicadas**, Lima, Peru; **CIBERTEC**, Peru; **National Research Technical University (MiSIS)**, Moscow, Russia; **Institut Obert de Catalunya (IOC)**, Barcelona, Spain; Sedat Çilingir, Burcu Tezcan, and Didem Mutçalıoğlu from **İstanbul Bilgi Üniversitesi**, Istanbul, Turkey.

Touchstone Second Edition authors and publishers would also like to thank the following contributors to *Touchstone Second Edition*:

Sue Aldcorn, Frances Amrani, Deborah Gordon, Lisa Hutchins, Nancy Jordan, Steven Kirk, Genevieve Kocienda, Linda-Marie Koza, Geraldine Mark, Julianna Nielsen, Kathryn O'Dell, Nicola Prentis, Ellen Shaw, Kristin Sherman, Luis Silva Susa, Mary Vaughn, Kerry S. Vrabel, Shari Young, and Eric Zuarino.

Authors' Acknowledgments

The authors would like to thank all the Cambridge University Press staff and freelancers who were involved in the creation of *Touchstone Second Edition*. In addition, they would like to acknowledge a huge debt of gratitude that they owe to two people: Mary Vaughn, for her role in creating *Touchstone First Edition* and for being a constant source of wisdom ever since, and Bryan Fletcher, who also had the vision that has led to the success of *Touchstone Blended Learning*.

Helen Sandiford would like to thank her family for their love and support, especially her husband Bryan.

The author team would also like to thank each other, for the joy of working together, sharing the same professional dedication, and for the mutual support and friendship.

Finally, the authors would like to thank our dear friend Alejandro Martinez, Global Training Manager, who sadly passed away in 2012. He is greatly missed by all who had the pleasure to work with him. Alex was a huge supporter of *Touchstone* and everyone is deeply grateful to him for his contribution to its success.

Touchstone Level 3B Contents and learning outcomes

	Learning outcomes	Language		
		Grammar	Vocabulary	Pronunciation
Unit 7 Relationships pages 65–74	• Talk about your circle of friends using relative clauses • Talk about dating using phrasal verbs • Soften comments with expressions like *sort of* • Use *though* to give a contrasting idea • Read an article about online dating • Write an article about your circle of friends	• Subject relative clauses • Object relative clauses • Phrasal verbs ***Extra practice***	• Phrasal verbs, including expressions to talk about relationships	***Speaking naturally*** • Stress in phrasal verbs ***Sounds right*** • Which sound in each group is different?
Unit 8 What if? pages 75–84	• Talk about wishes and imaginary situations using *I wish* and *If* clauses • Discuss how to deal with everyday dilemmas • Give advice using expressions like *If I were you,* . . . • Use *That would be* . . . to comment on a suggestion or a possibility • Read a blog about regrets • Write an article about how you would change your life	• Use *wish* + past form of verb to talk about wishes for the present or future • Conditional sentences with *if* clauses about imaginary situations • Asking about imaginary situations or events ***Extra practice***	• Expressions with verbs and prepositions	***Speaking naturally*** • Intonation in long questions ***Sounds right*** • Are these sounds the same or different?
Unit 9 Tech savvy? pages 85–94	• Talk about problems with technology using questions within sentences • Ask for help and describe how things work using *how to, where to, what to,* and separable phrasal verbs • Give different opinions with expressions like *On the other hand,* . . . • Ask someone to agree with you using expressions like *You know what I mean?* • Read an article about email scams • Write an article about protecting personal information	• Questions within sentences • Separable phrasal verbs with objects • *how to* + verb, *where to* + verb, and *what to* + verb ***Extra practice***	• Phrasal verbs, including expressions to talk about operating electronic machines and gadgets	***Speaking naturally*** • Linking consonants and vowels ***Sounds right*** • Identifying unstressed syllables
Checkpoint Units 7–9 pages 95–96				
Unit 10 What's up? pages 97–106	• Talk about news with the present perfect continuous, present perfect, *since, for,* and *in* • Use the present perfect with *already, still,* and *yet* • Describe different kinds of movies • Ask someone for a favor politely • Use *All right, OK,* and *Sure* to agree to requests • Use *All right, OK,* and *So* to change topic • Read a movie review • Write a review	• Present perfect continuous vs. present perfect • *Since, for,* and *in* for duration • *Already, still,* and *yet* with present perfect ***Extra practice***	• Kinds of movies • Expressions to describe types of movies	***Speaking naturally*** • Reduction of *have* ***Sounds right*** • Matching vowel sounds
Unit 11 Impressions pages 107–116	• Speculate about people and things using *must, might, can't,* and *could* • Describe situations and people's feelings using adjectives that end in *-ed* and *-ing* • Show you understand situations or feelings • Use *you see* to explain a situation and *I see* to show you understand • Read an article about a music education program • Write an email to the founder of a charity	• Modal verbs *must, may, might, can't,* or *could* for speculating • Adjectives ending in *-ed* vs. adjectives ending in *-ing* ***Extra practice***	• Feelings and reactions	***Speaking naturally*** • Linking and deletion with *must* ***Sounds right*** • *-ed* adjective endings
Unit 12 In the news pages 117–126	• Talk about news events using the simple past passive • Talk about natural disasters using the simple past passive + *by* • Use expressions like *Guess what?* to tell news • Introduce ideas with expressions like *The thing is* . . . • Read an interview with a foreign correspondent • Write a report using statistics	• The simple past passive • The simple past passive with *by* + agent • Adverbs with the passive ***Extra practice***	• Extreme weather conditions • Natural disasters	***Speaking naturally*** • Breaking sentences into parts ***Sounds right*** • Matching words that have the same sounds
Checkpoint Units 10–12 pages 127–128				

iv

Interaction	Skills				Self study
Conversation strategies	Listening	Reading	Writing	Free talk	Vocabulary notebook
• Soften comments with expressions like *I think*, *probably*, *kind of*, and *in a way* • Use *though* to give a contrasting idea	***People I look forward to seeing*** • Listen to someone describe three people; listen for the reasons he likes to see them ***Getting back in touch*** • Listen to a conversation about losing touch and fill in a chart	***Looking for love? Online is the way to go!*** • Read an article about online dating	***Your circle of friends*** • Write an article describing your circle of friends • Use *both* and *neither* to show what you have in common	***Your ideal partner*** • Group work: Discuss your ideal partner and questions you should ask before you decide to get married	***Matching up*** • When you learn a phrasal verb, it's a good idea to write down some other verbs you can use with the particle and some other particles you can use with the verb
• Give advice using expressions like *If I were you, . . .* and *You might want to . . .* • Use *That would be . . .* to comment on a suggestion or possibility	***Just one wish*** • Identify four people's wishes; then write the reasons they can't have their wishes ***Here's my advice*** • Listen to a conversation about problems and advice	***If I could live my live over . . .*** • Read a blog about regrets	***What would you change?*** • Write an article about how you would change your life • Use adverbs like *probably* and *definitely* in affirmative and negative statements	***What would you do?*** • Group work: Discuss what you would do in imaginary situations	***Imagine that!*** • When you learn a new verb, find out what prepositions (if any) can come after it
• Give different opinions using expressions like *On the other hand . . .* and *I know what you mean, but . . .* • Use expressions like *You know what I mean?* when you want someone to agree with you	***What do you know about the Internet?*** • Answer questions about the Internet; then listen to a conversation and check your answers ***Technology matters*** • Listen to a conversation about the pros and cons of technology; then agree or disagree with three opinions	***Savvy and safe*** • Read an article about email scams	***Keeping it safe*** • Write an article about protecting personal information • Planning your article	***Technology etiquette*** • Pair work: Debate different opinions about technology etiquette	***On and off*** • When you learn expressions with a new or complex structure, think of everyday situations where you might use them

Checkpoint Units 7–9   pages 95–96

• Ask for a favor politely using expressions like *I was wondering . . .* and *Would it be OK with you . . .* • Use *All right*, *OK*, and *Sure* to agree to requests and *All right*, *OK*, and *So* to move a conversation to a new topic	***Favors at work*** • Match people with the favors they ask; then listen again for more information ***I'd really recommend it*** • Listen for details of a conversation about going to see a show	***Avatar is stunning, memorable, and mesmerizing!*** • Read a movie review	***A Review*** • Write a review of a concert, show, movie, or book • Contrast ideas with *although*, *even though*, and *even if*	***Who's been doing what?*** • Class activity: Ask questions to find out interesting things your classmates have been doing lately	***Great movies*** • When you learn a new word or expression, link it to something you have recently seen or done
• Show you understand another person's feelings or situation • Use *you see* to explain a situation • Use *I see* to show you understand	***People and situations*** • Match four people and their situations; then write a response with *must* to each ***People making a difference*** • Listen for details of conversations about people and organizations; discuss which organization you would choose to get involved with	***El Sistema*** • Read an article about a music education program	***My impression is . . .*** • Write an email to the founder of a charity • Expressions to show impressions, reactions, and opinions	***That must be fun!*** • Pair work: Make sentences to share with a partner. Then continue the conversation and speculate about what they say.	***How would you feel?*** • When you learn new words for feelings, link them to different situations where you might experience each one
• Introduce news with expressions like *Did you hear (about) . . . ?* and *Guess what?* • Use *The thing is / was . . .* to introduce issues	***News update*** • Listen to news stories and answer questions ***What do they say next?*** • Listen to people telling personal news and make predictions	***Life's work: Christiane Amanpour*** • Read an interview with a foreign correspondent	***Are you up on the news?*** • Write a report using statistics • Writing about statistics	***Here's the news!*** • Pair work: Make up short TV news reports about pictures and take turns telling news stories to another pair.	***Forces of nature*** • When you learn a new word, use a dictionary to find out what other words are typically used with it

Checkpoint Units 10–12   pages 127–128

Useful language for . . .

Working in groups

Does anyone else have anything to add?

What do you think, _____ ?

Let's take turns asking the questions.
OK, who wants to go first?

Do you want me to make the list?

Should I write down the information this time?

Do you have any ideas?

Do you know what the answer is?

We're going to do a role play about . . .

In our survey, we found out that . . .

We agreed on these things. First, . . .

We're finished. What should we do next?

Checking your partner's work

Can you help me with this question? I'm stuck.

I can't figure out this answer. Can you help me?

Would you mind checking my work?

Let's compare answers.

Let's exchange papers.

I can't read your writing. What does this say?

I'm not sure what you mean.
Do you mean _____ ?

I don't understand what this means.
Are you trying to say _____ ?

Your blog was really interesting. I just wanted
to ask you a question about _____ .

I was wondering about _____ .

Relationships

UNIT **7**

✓ **Can Do!** In this unit, you learn how to . . .

Lesson A
- Talk about your circle of friends using relative clauses

Lesson B
- Talk about dating using phrasal verbs like *get along* and *break up*

Lesson C
- Use expressions like *probably* and *sort of* to soften comments
- Use *though* to give a contrasting idea

Lesson D
- Read an article about online dating
- Write an article describing your circle of friends

1

2

3

4

What relationships do you have with other people?
Are you a friend to someone? a family member? a co-worker?
Which relationships do you enjoy most?

65

CHRISTOPHER OWEN

talks about his circle of friends.

My running buddy . . .
"Well, Mike is the guy I run with in the morning. He's the one who got me started running when I was in college. It's convenient because he lives right down the street."

My most exciting friend . . .
"Jennifer is another friend from college. Jen plays in a rock band that's really hot right now, so her life is very different from mine. She still calls a lot to talk about all the things she's doing. That's kind of fun."

My oldest friend . . .
"Charlie is someone I grew up with. We've been through a lot together. I can tell him just about anything. He's just someone I can totally trust."

My roommate . . .
"Yuya is a guy that Jen introduced me to. He was looking for an apartment to share. It's great because he's a 'clean freak.' I've never lived in a place that's so clean."

A new friend . . .
"Then there's Angela. She's a new friend I met through Mike. She's cool. She's the kind of person you can just call and say, 'You want to go see a movie tonight?' That kind of thing."

A friend from work . . .
"Nina is an interesting woman who sits across from me at work. She used to have a company that planned weddings for people. She has some funny stories to tell."

 Getting started

A Where do people make friends? How many places can you think of? Make a list.

B ◀)) 3.01 Listen and read the article above. How did Christopher meet his friends?

Figure it out **C** How does Christopher express these ideas? Underline the sentences in the article.

1. Nina is an interesting woman. She sits across from me at work.
2. Jen plays in a rock band. It's really hot right now.
3. Angela is a new friend. I met her through Mike.
4. Jen calls me a lot to talk about things. She's doing a lot of things.

Grammar Relative clauses 🔊 **3.02**

Extra practice p. 146

> Relative clauses begin with *who*, *that*, and *which*. They give information about people
> or things. Use *who* and *that* to refer to people and *that* and *which* to refer to things.
>
> **Subject relative clauses**
> *Who*, *that*, *which* are the subject of the verb.
> Nina is an interesting woman **who / that sits across from me**.
> Nina used to have a company **that / which planned weddings**.
>
> **Object relative clauses**
> *Who*, *that*, *which* are the object of the verb.
> Charlie is someone (**who / that**) **I can trust**.   (**I can trust** Charlie.)
> Jen talks about the things (**that**) **she's doing**.   (**Jen's doing** things.)

In conversation

In subject relative clauses:
- *Who* is more common than *that* for people.
- *That* is more common than *which* for things.

In object relative clauses:
- People often leave out *who* and *that*, especially before pronouns.
- *Which* is not frequent.

A Combine each pair of sentences using relative clauses.
   More than one answer may be possible.

1. I have a really good friend. She works at a local radio station.

   _____

2. There was a really funny guy in my high school. He was always telling jokes.

   _____

3. One of my friends from class has a football. His favorite team signed it.

   _____

4. My best friend has a really pretty gold ring. Her grandfather gave it to her.

   _____

5. I have a new friend. I met him in my kickboxing class.

   _____

6. My friend and I saw a movie last night. It made us both cry.

   _____

Common errors

Don't use pronouns that repeat ideas in relative clauses.

*Janet has a company **that makes** toys.* (NOT . . . *company that ~~it~~ makes toys*.)

*She's a friend **that I met** through Mike.* (NOT . . . *friend that I met ~~her~~ through Mike.*)

About you **B** **Pair work** Make five true sentences about people you know. Take turns telling a partner.
   Ask questions to find out more information.

   A I have a really good friend who works for an airline.
   B Really? Which airline?

3 **Talk about it** Who's in your circle of friends?

Group work Discuss the questions. Give as much information as you can.

▸ Who's your closest friend? How did you meet?

▸ How many friends do you have on your social networking site?

▸ Do you have any friends that you only contact occasionally?

▸ Who were your friends when you were growing up?

▸ Are you still in touch with the friends that you grew up with?

▸ Do you have any friends that have exciting lives? Explain why.

▸ Do you have any friends who are very different from you? How are they different?

Building vocabulary and grammar

A ◀))) **3.03** Put the story in the correct order. Number the parts from 1 to 6. Then listen and check your answers.

HIGH SCHOOL SWEETHEARTS ♡♡♡♡♡♡♡♡♡♡♡♡

☐ He discovered that Anna was a member. He wrote her an email, and she **wrote back** right away. It **turned out** that Anna was still single and was looking for him, too! They made plans to meet at a restaurant in her city.

☐ Steve and Anna **grew up** in a small town called Greenville. In high school, they **hung out** with the same crowd. They **got along** very well, and they started **going out** together. Anna was Steve's first love, and he was her first love, too.

☐ When Steve was 35, he was ready to **settle down** with someone, but no one seemed right. He still thought about Anna. Then he heard about a website that helps find old classmates. He signed up immediately.

☐ But the long-distance relationship didn't **work out**, and they decided to **break up**. A year later, Anna's family **moved away** from Greenville, and Steve lost touch with her.

Anna and Steve at their high school prom

A recent photo of the happy couple

☐ When they saw each other, all the old memories **came back**, and they started **going out** again. Within a few months they were married, and they are now living "happily ever after." Sometimes your first love **turns out** to be the best.

☐ After they graduated, Anna **went away** to college, while Steve attended a college nearby. They would get together about once a month, when Anna **flew back** home to visit her parents.

Figure it out **B** Which verbs in the story mean the same as the underlined expressions below?

1. Steve and Anna <u>spent their childhood</u> in the same town.
2. Steve and Anna started <u>dating</u>.
3. Anna <u>went somewhere else</u> to college.
4. Steve and Anna decided to <u>stop dating</u>

Word sort **C** Complete the chart with phrasal verbs from the story. Then take turns retelling the story with a partner. How many verbs can you use?

along	away	back	down	up	out
		write back			

📓 **Vocabulary notebook** p. 74

2 **Grammar** Phrasal verbs 🔊 3.04

Extra practice p. 146

A phrasal verb is a verb plus a particle like *along*, *away*, *back*, *out*, *up*, etc.

Steve and Anna **grew up** in the same town.
They **got along** well and started **going out** together.
Anna **went away** to college.
She **flew back** home once a month.
Things didn't **work out**, so they decided to **break up**.

Notice

Steve and Anna **got along** well.
Steve **got along with** Anna.
Anna **got along with** Steve.
Steve and Anna **went out** together.
Steve **went out with** Anna.
Anna **went out with** Steve.

A Complete the opinions with the phrasal verbs in the box.

break up	go back	move away	sign up	work out
get along	✓go out	settle down	turn out	write back

1. It's more fun to _____*go out*_____ with someone you know than to go on a "blind date."

2. If you don't _____ well with your boyfriend's or girlfriend's family, your relationship won't _____ .

3. It's good to date a lot of different people before you _____ with one person.

4. After you _____ with someone, you should try and stay friends.

5. You should never _____ to someone you've broken up with.

6. If you want to meet someone, it's a good idea to _____ for a class.

7. First dates usually _____ to be a disaster!

8. Relationships never work out when one person has to _____ .

9. When a close friend sends you an email, you should _____ immediately.

About you **B** **Pair work** Discuss the opinions above. Do you agree?

3 **Speaking naturally** Stress in phrasal verbs

Are you going out with anyone?   *How are you getting along?*

A 🔊 3.05 Listen and repeat the questions above. Notice that in phrasal verbs the particle is stressed more than the verb.

B 🔊 3.06 Listen and repeat the questions below. Underline the stressed particles.

1. Do you think it's OK to go out with more than one person at the same time?

2. What should you do if you're not getting along with your boyfriend or girlfriend?

3. Do you think relationships can work out if you work in the same place?

4. Is it OK to go out with someone who is a lot older or younger than you?

5. What's a good age to settle down?

6. What's the best way to break up with someone?

About you **C** **Group work** Ask and answer the questions. How many different opinions do you have?

1 Conversation strategy   Softening comments

A What are your neighbors like? Do you get along with them? Tell the class.

B 🔊 3.07 Listen. What does Olivia think about her new neighbor?
What are Adam's neighbors like?

Olivia	That woman by the mailboxes – she just moved in next door.
Adam	Yeah? She seems pretty friendly.
Olivia	She's OK. She's a little bit strange, though.
Adam	Yeah? How do you mean?
Olivia	Well, it's kind of weird. She's always coming over and borrowing things from me.
Adam	She's probably just a little lonely or something.
Olivia	Yeah. Maybe she is. But then other times she sort of ignores me. She's just a bit odd, I guess.
Adam	Yeah, in my building nobody ever speaks. I mean, we all smile but we don't really know each other.
Olivia	I guess that's OK in a way, though. I don't like to get too friendly with the neighbors.
Adam	Me either.

C Notice how Olivia and Adam use these expressions to "soften" their comments. Find examples in the conversation.

I guess / I think	*a little / a (little) bit*
probably / maybe	*just*
kind of / sort of	*in a way*

D Make the comments below softer. Add the expressions given.

1. The people in my neighborhood are unfriendly. (a little)
   They're just busy with their own lives. (maybe)

2. The people next door keep to themselves. (kind of)
   They don't like to go out. (I guess)

3. The people across the street are always looking out of their window. They seem nosy. (a little)
   They don't have anything better to do. (I guess)

4. The guy above me plays his music too loud. (a bit) It gets noisy. (kind of)
   It can be difficult to sleep. (a little bit)

5. One of my neighbors is always coming over. It's irritating. (in a way)
   She's lonely. (I think / probably / just)

About you **E** **Pair work** Do you know anyone like the people above? Take turns telling a partner.
Can you "soften" your comments?

"Actually, the woman in our local store is a little unfriendly. She's not very helpful."

2 Strategy plus *though*

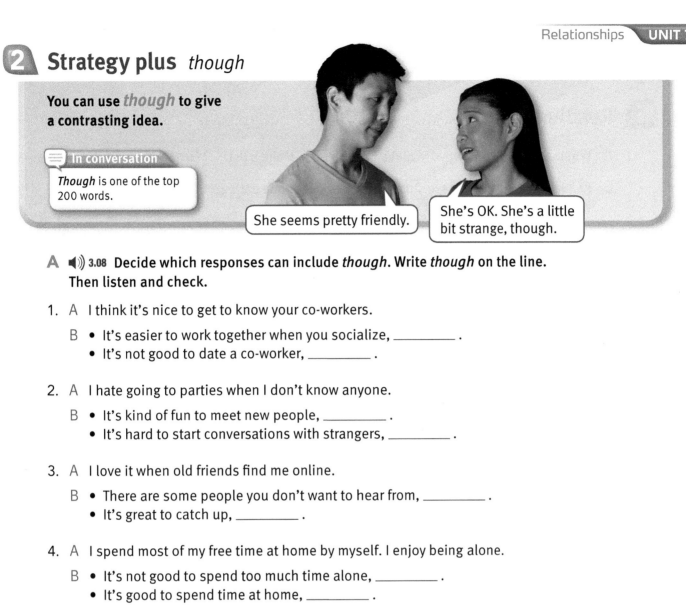

**You can use *though* to give
a contrasting idea.**

In conversation

Though is one of the top
200 words.

She seems pretty friendly.

She's OK. She's a little
bit strange, though.

A ◀)) **3.08 Decide which responses can include *though*. Write *though* on the line.
Then listen and check.**

1. A I think it's nice to get to know your co-workers.

    B • It's easier to work together when you socialize, _____ .
       • It's not good to date a co-worker, _____ .

2. A I hate going to parties when I don't know anyone.

    B • It's kind of fun to meet new people, _____ .
       • It's hard to start conversations with strangers, _____ .

3. A I love it when old friends find me online.

    B • There are some people you don't want to hear from, _____ .
       • It's great to catch up, _____ .

4. A I spend most of my free time at home by myself. I enjoy being alone.

    B • It's not good to spend too much time alone, _____ .
       • It's good to spend time at home, _____ .

About you **B** **Pair work Practice the conversations above. Then practice again giving your own responses.**

3 Listening and strategies People I look forward to seeing

A ◀)) **3.09 Listen to Matthew talk about three people he looks forward to seeing.
Complete the sentences.**

1. The woman in the coffee shop gets a little _____ .
    She's really _____ and positive, though.

2. My yoga teacher is really good. He's kind of _____ , though.
    The other students are nice. One guy is always _____ , though.
    It gets sort of _____ .

3. One of the guys that I go biking with is the worst biker.
    He's incredibly _____ , though. I guess the other guys are kind
    of _____ about biking.

B ◀)) **3.09 Listen again. Why does Matthew look forward to seeing each person?**

About you **C** **Pair work Who do you look forward to seeing? Tell a partner about
three people. Ask and answer questions to find out more information.**

((• Sounds right p. 138

Reading

A **What are some good ways to make new friends? Make a list.**

B **Read the article. What have studies found about online dating? What are the reasons for its popularity?**

> **Reading tip**
>
> Writers often use different ways to present statistics, like *20 percent, one in five,* or *one out of (every) five.*

---

http://www.looking...   🔍

LOOKING FOR LOVE? Online is the way to go!

According to new research, people looking for romance need look no further than their laptops. Recent studies reveal that 17 percent of marriages are the result of an initial online encounter – making this the second most common way of meeting a potential partner, after meeting through friends.

Surveys show that more than one-third of singles looking for a partner have used an online dating site. Furthermore, one out of every five new relationships starts online. Although the results of online dating surveys may vary, the evidence points to the increasingly important role the Internet is playing in helping single people find romance.

The social stigma[1] that was attached to online dating in the past is fast disappearing as dating goes increasingly digital. These days, most people know someone who has tried online dating, so people are less afraid to talk about it or to try it. Online dating, it appears, has entered the mainstream.

But why is this? Experts say there are several factors that contribute to the popularity of online dating. Changes in lifestyle, geographic mobility, and the rise in social networking are largely responsible for changing how people meet potential partners. These days, people typically delay marriage as they concentrate on their careers, work longer and longer hours, and live farther away from family and childhood friends who might otherwise provide contacts with eligible[2] partners. Instead they turn to their tablets.

So has the Internet fundamentally changed *how* people date? According to Greg Blatt, former CEO of a popular dating website, the answer is no. "This is just meeting," Blatt says. "It's no different meeting on a dating website than it is meeting at a party, or at a restaurant, or on a subway. . . . Once you've met, it's real life; you either fall for each other, or you don't. You either have a great romance, or you don't."

"Computers are not taking the place of romance," he says. "They're just another way to put yourself in a position to meet somebody with a chance for romance."

1. *(a) stigma*: a bad opinion of someone or something
2. *eligible*: ideal as a marriage partner

C **Read the article again. Circle the correct words to make the sentences true according to the article.**

1. Seventeen percent of people who get married now meet **on the Internet / through friends.**

2. Meeting people through friends is **more / less** common than meeting online.

3. A third of people looking for romance **don't use / use** dating websites.

4. Online dating is now considered more **acceptable /dangerous.**

5. One reason why people try online dating is because they live farther away from their **place of work / original community.**

6. Blatt says that meeting online is **like / not like** meeting at an actual place, such as a party.

About you D **Pair work** Discuss the opinions expressed in the article. Which do you agree with? Why?

2 Speaking and listening Getting back in touch

A Pair work How do friends lose touch with each other? Add ideas to the list. Have you ever lost touch with a friend? Tell your partner how it happened.

Friends lose touch when one of them . . .
- moves away.
- gets married.
- gets interested in different things.
- gets too busy with school or work.
- _____ .
- _____ .

B 🔊 3.10 Listen to Javier talk about his old friends. Does he want to get back in touch with them? Check (✓) the correct boxes in the chart below.

	Yes	No	Don't know	Why did he lose touch?
1. His college friends	☐	☐	☐	_____
2. His running buddy	☐	☐	☐	_____
3. His old girlfriend	☐	☐	☐	_____

C 🔊 3.10 Listen again. Why did Javier lose touch with his friends? Complete the rest of the chart.

3 Writing Your circle of friends

A Pair work Think about three of your friends. Tell a partner about them. Discuss the questions below.

- What is your friend like?
- How did you meet?
- Why did you become friends?
- What do you have in common?
- What do you do together?

B Read the article below and the Help note. Then write an article like the one on page 66 about your circle of friends. Use *both* and *neither* to show what you have in common. Include photos if you can.

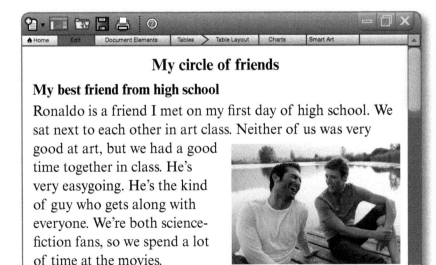

My circle of friends

My best friend from high school

Ronaldo is a friend I met on my first day of high school. We sat next to each other in art class. Neither of us was very good at art, but we had a good time together in class. He's very easygoing. He's the kind of guy who gets along with everyone. We're both science-fiction fans, so we spend a lot of time at the movies.

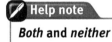
Help note

Both and ***neither***

We're **both** science-fiction fans. **Both of us** are science-fiction fans.

We **both** like going to the movies. **Both of us** like going to the movies.

Neither of us was very good at art.

C Pair work Read your partner's article. Ask questions about your partner's friends.

Free talk p. 132

73

Learning tip *Phrasal verbs*

When you learn a phrasal verb, it's a good idea to write down

- some other verbs you can use with the particle.

  back: get back / call back / fly back

- some other particles you can use with the verb.

  go: go back / go out / go away

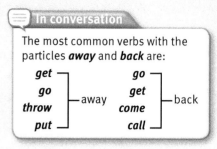

In conversation

The most common verbs with the particles *away* and *back* are:

get		*go*	
go	—away	*get*	—back
throw		*come*	
put		*call*	

1 Circle the two verbs in each list that go with the particle on the right.

1. go / move / hang   **away**
2. wake / eat / work   **out**

3. come / break / get   **back**
4. wake / go / come   **over**

5. sign / grow / sleep   **up**
6. fall / eat / settle   **down**

2 Complete each expression with a different verb.

wake				
	in the morning			with your friends
	for a class			late
up	without an alarm clock		**out**	to a club
	in a small town			at a nice restaurant
	with your boyfriend / girlfriend			at the gym

3 **Word builder** How many new phrasal verbs can you make from these particles?

away   back   down   out   up

 On your own

Make lists with headings for different topics such as "Relationships" or "Going out." Write phrasal verbs for each topic, and learn the words whenever you have a minute.

Relationships:
- work out
- get along
- break up

 Can Do! Now I can . . .

✓ I can . . .   ? I need to review how to . . .

- [ ] describe people and things using relative clauses.
- [ ] talk about friends and romantic relationships.
- [ ] soften comments with expressions like *sort of.*
- [ ] use *though* to give contrasting ideas.
- [ ] understand descriptions of people.

- [ ] understand a conversation about old friends.
- [ ] understand someone talking about losing touch with people.
- [ ] read an article about online dating.
- [ ] write about my circle of friends.

What if?

✓ Can Do! In this unit, you learn how to . . .

Lesson A
- Talk about wishes using *I wish* + past form
- Talk about imaginary situations or events in the present and the future with *If*-clauses

Lesson B
- Discuss how to deal with everyday dilemmas
- Ask about imaginary situations or events

Lesson C
- Give advice using expressions like *If I were you, . . .* or *I'd . . .*
- Use *That would be . . .* to comment on a suggestion or a possibility

Lesson D
- Read a blog about regrets
- Write an article about how you would change your life

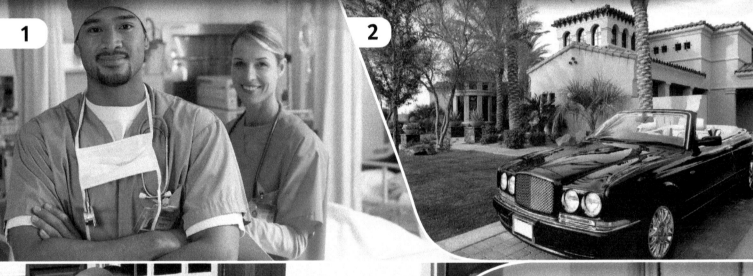

1

2

3

4

What are your priorities in life? Rank these things in order from 1 (most important) to 6 (least important).

- ☐ your health
- ☐ your career
- ☐ wealth
- ☐ your family
- ☐ relationships
- ☐ looking good

What other things matter to you?

How do you wish your life were different?

"I just wish I weren't so busy with my work. I have to work most weekends, so I never have enough time to do anything fun. If I had more free time, I'd go kayaking every weekend."

– Berta Palmas, Monterrey

"We just got married, and we're renting a tiny little apartment. It would be great if we could afford a bigger place to live. We don't have enough room for all our stuff."

– Min Sup and Jin Eun Cho, Seoul

"Well, I never get to go away on holiday. I just don't have enough money. So I wish I had enough money to go somewhere exciting. Yeah, if I could choose anywhere, I'd probably go to Egypt to see the pyramids. That would be great!"

– Bryan Gibson, Melbourne

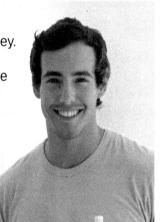

"I wish I didn't live so far away from my family. My sister just had a baby – a little boy – and I never get to see him. I really miss everyone. If I lived closer, I'd be able to help out."

– Irene Chang, Taipei

1 Getting started

A **What would you like more of in your life? Tell the class.**

fun   money   time   vacations   work

B 🔊 **3.11 Listen to the people above talk about their wishes. What do they want?**

Figure it out **C** **Circle the correct verbs in the sentences below. Use the article above to help you. Then answer the questions. What do you notice about the verbs you circled?**

1. Bryan wishes he **has** / **had** enough money to go away. Does he have enough money?

2. Berta says, "I just wish **I'm not** / **weren't** so busy." Is she busy now?

3. Irene says if she **lives** / **lived** closer, she would help her sister. Does she live close?

4. Min Sup and Jin Eun say it **would** / **will** be great if they could rent a big apartment. What's their place like?

2 Grammar Wishes and imaginary situations or events ◀)) 3.12

Extra practice p. 147

Wishes for the present or future	Imaginary situations or events in the present or future
wish + past form of verb	*If* + past form of verb . . . *would* (*could*) + verb

I wish I **had** more free time. ▶ If I **had** more free time, I'**d** / I **would go** kayaking.
(I **don't have** enough free time, so I **don't go** kayaking.)

She wishes she **didn't live** so far away. ▶ If she **lived** closer, she'**d** / she **would be able to** help out.
(She **lives** very far away so she **isn't able to** help out.)

I wish I **weren't** so busy with my work. ▶ If I **were** less busy, I **could go away** on the weekends.
(I'**m** very busy with my work, so I **can't go away** on the weekends.)

We wish we **could afford** to move. ▶ If we **could afford** to move, we **wouldn't live** in this tiny place.
(We **can't afford** to move, so we **live** in this tiny place.)

A Complete the sentences with the appropriate form of the verbs given.

1. I wish I ___could do___ (can do) something more exciting with my life. If I ___had___ (have) the chance, I ___would travel___ (travel) around South America.

2. I wish I _____ (not be) so shy. If I _____ (have) more confidence, I _____ probably _____ (enjoy) going out more.

3. I wish I _____ (not have to) study so hard. If I _____ (not get) so much homework, I _____ (be able to) play on the soccer team.

4. I wish _____ (can finish) my degree this year. If I _____ (graduate) this year, I _____ (can get) a job, and I _____ (can start) to pay off my student loans.

5. I wish I _____ (can find) a job nearer to home. If I _____ (get) a new job, maybe I _____ (not have to) commute two hours a day.

6. I wish I _____ (be) famous. If I _____ (be) famous, I _____ (be able to) go to shows and get the best seats! And I _____ (not eat) in the cheapest restaurants anymore.

In conversation

People say *I wish I was . . .* and *If I was . . .* more frequently than *I wish I were . . .* and *If I were . . .*, but this is not considered correct in written English.

█████████ *I wish I was . . .*
██ *I wish I were . . .*

Common errors

Use the simple past form after *if*.
*If we **had** more money, we could go on vacation more often.* (NOT *If we would have* more . . .)

About you **B** **Pair work** Discuss the sentences above. Do you have any wishes like these?

"I wish I could do something more exciting. If I had the chance, I would live in another country."

3 Listening and speaking Just one wish

A ◀)) 3.13 Listen to four people talk about their wishes. Complete the sentences.

What do they wish for?	Why can't they have their wish?
1. Daniel wishes _____ .	_____
2. Martine wishes _____ .	_____
3. Miguel wishes _____ .	_____
4. Mi Yun wishes _____ .	_____

B ◀)) 3.13 Listen again. Why can't they have their wishes? Write the reason(s) above.

About you **C** **Class activity** Ask your classmates about their wishes. What are the most popular wishes?

1 Building vocabulary and grammar

 About you **A** 🔊 **3.14** Listen and take the quiz. Circle your answers. Then compare with a partner.

WHAT WOULD YOU DO?

1. What would you do if a friend accidentally spilled coffee all over your phone, and it stopped working? Would you . . .
   a. let your friend buy a new one?
   b. tell your friend not to **worry about** it and **buy** a new phone **for** yourself?

2. What would you do if you **borrowed** a camera **from** a friend and broke it? Would you . . .
   a. simply **apologize for** breaking it?
   b. take it to a store and **pay for** the repairs?

3. How would you react if a friend started dating someone you used to go out with? Would you . . .
   a. **talk to** your friend **about** your feelings?
   b. feel hurt but **say** nothing **to** either of them?

4. What would you do if a friend came for dinner and brought an expensive box of chocolates? Would you . . .
   a. **thank** your friend **for** the gift and not open it?
   b. **share** the chocolates **with** your friend after dinner?

5. What would you say if a friend **asked** you **for** a loan to buy a new laptop? Would you say . . . ?
   a. "Sorry, I never **lend** money **to** anyone."
   b. "I'll **think about** it and let you know."

6. What would you do if a friend borrowed $10 and forgot to pay you back? Would you . . .
   a. **remind** your friend **about** it several times?
   b. **forget about** it?

Word sort **B** **Pair work** Write the prepositions that are used in the quiz in the expressions below. Then ask and answer the questions with a partner.

1. What do you worry *about* ?
2. Who do you talk to _____ problems?
3. Do you ever think _____ your diet?
4. How do you remind yourself _____ things?
5. Can you forget _____ your problems?
6. Do you buy gifts _____ your friends?
7. Do you use cash to pay _____ things?
8. Do you apologize _____ being late?
9. How do you thank people _____ gifts?
10. Did you ask a friend _____ a favor today?
11. Do you borrow clothes _____ friends?
12. Do you lend books _____ friends?
13. What can't you say no _____ ?
14. Do you ever share secrets _____ friends?

Figure it out **C** Complete these questions about imaginary situations. Use the quiz to help you. Then ask and answer the questions in pairs.

Vocabulary notebook p. 84

1. What _____ you _____ (do) if your friend _____ (forget) your birthday?
2. How _____ you _____ (react) if a friend _____ (tell) everyone a secret about you?

2 Speaking naturally Intonation in long questions

How would you react if a friend started dating someone you used to go out with?

What would you do if a friend came for dinner and brought an expensive box of chocolates?

A 🔊 **3.15** Listen and repeat the questions above. Notice how the intonation falls and then rises to show the question is not finished and then falls at the end.

About you **B** **Pair work** Find a partner. Take turns asking the questions in the quiz on page 78 and giving your own answers. Pay attention to the intonation of the long questions.

3 Grammar Asking about imaginary situations or events 🔊 3.16

Extra practice p. 147

What **would** you **do if** you **broke** a friend's camera?
  I'd apologize for breaking it.
  I'd pay for the repairs.
  I **wouldn't say** anything about it.

Would you **pay** for a new one?
  Yes, I **would**. / No, I **wouldn't**.

A Make questions with *would* using the ideas below. Compare with a partner.

1. a friend is 15 minutes late / call and remind him about it
   What would you do if a friend was 15 minutes late? Would you call and remind him about it?

2. you hear a strange noise in the middle of the night / go and see what it was
   _____

3. a salesperson charges you the wrong price for something / say something to her
   _____

4. you scratch a car with a shopping cart in a parking lot / leave a note with your name and number
   _____

5. you find a nice pair of gloves on the sidewalk / think about keeping them
   _____

6. you have an extra ticket for a show / offer it to a friend but ask him to pay for it
   _____

7. you get a gift that you hate from a friend / thank her for it and then get rid of it
   _____

8. your friend asks for help moving into an apartment / find an excuse to get out of helping him
   _____

9. your friend is in a bad mood / take him out for a fun night
   _____

About you **B** **Pair work** Take turns asking the questions above. Discuss your answers. Do you agree?

  A What would you do if a friend was 15 minutes late for a date?
  B I'd probably just wait a little longer. Would you call and remind him about it?

1 Conversation strategy Giving advice

A What tough decisions have you made? Did you ask for advice? Tell the class.

B ◀)) 3.17 Listen. What advice does Nicole give Carlos about grad school?

Nicole Hey, I hear you got accepted to grad school.

Carlos Yeah. I got into MSU and Bracken Tech.

Nicole Congratulations! So where are you going to go?

Carlos I don't know. I got a full scholarship to Bracken Tech, but I think MSU has a better engineering department.

Nicole Well, if I were you, I'd take the scholarship. Then you wouldn't have to borrow any money.

Carlos Yeah, that would be great. But it's a tough decision.

Nicole Well, Bracken Tech's a good school. I mean, you might want to go there and meet some of the professors.

Carlos That'd be good. But then, everybody I know is going to MSU.

Nicole Oh, I wouldn't worry about that. You can make new friends. And anyway, I might go to Bracken next year, you know, if I get accepted.

Carlos Really? That would be awesome!

C **Notice** how Nicole gives advice to Carlos. She uses expressions like these. Find examples in the conversation.

If I were you, I'd . . .   *You might want to . . .*
I would / I'd . . .   *You could . . .*
I wouldn't . . .

About you **D** **Pair work** Think of three pieces of advice for each problem below. Then take turns role-playing the problems and giving advice.

1. I wish I weren't majoring in economics. I just don't find it very interesting.
2. One of my co-workers just got a promotion, but I didn't get one.
3. I wish I knew what to do after college.
4. My boyfriend / girlfriend wants to get married, but I'm just not ready.
5. My parents want me to study law or accounting or something, but I don't want to.

"Well, if I were you, I'd try and switch to a different major. . . . "

2 **Strategy plus** That would be . . .

You can use
That would be . . .
to comment on a
suggestion or a
possibility.

You might want to go there and meet some of the professors.

That'd be good.

I might go to Bracken next year.

Really? That would be awesome!

Complete the responses. Practice with a partner. Then take turns asking and answering the questions.

In conversation

The most frequent adjectives after *That would be . . .* are *nice*, *good*, *great*, *fun*, *cool*, *interesting*, *fine*, *wonderful*, *neat*, *hard*, and *awesome*.

1. A If you could do something really different, what would you do?

   B I'd really like to go skydiving.

   A Really? Wow! That would be _____ !

2. A If you could have any job, what would you do?

   B Something creative. I'd like to work in a design company or something.

   A Yeah. That'd be _____ .

3. A Would you ever like to get a Ph.D. in something?

   B Yeah, maybe one day. But it's impossible right now. I'm just too busy. I'd have to study at midnight!

   A Oh, yeah. That would be _____ .

3 **Listening and strategies** Here's my advice.

A ◀)) 3.18 Listen to Tom and Amy talk about their problems. What problems do they have? Complete the sentences on the left.

What's the problem?

1. Tom wishes he _____ .
2. Tom wishes his boss _____ .
3. One of Tom's co-workers got _____ .
4. Amy can't decide which school to go to because _____ .

What's the advice?

"I wouldn't _____ . You could _____ ."
"I would _____ ."
"If I were you, I'd _____ ."
"I wouldn't _____ ."

B ◀)) 3.18 Listen again. What advice do Tom and Amy give each other? Complete the sentences above.

C **Pair work** Choose one of Tom or Amy's problems, or one of your own.
Take turns describing the problem and offering advice.

   A *I have a similar problem to Tom. I have a part-time job that I really like, but it doesn't pay very well.*

   B *Well, maybe you could ask for a raise.*

   A *Yeah, that would be good.*

(((• Sounds right p. 138

81

1 Reading

A What kinds of things do people regret in life? Make a class list.

B Read the blog. What impression do you have of the writer (age, gender, personality)? Compare ideas with a partner.

Reading tip

As you read, try to imagine the situations, places, or people that the writer describes.

IF I COULD LIVE MY LIFE OVER . . .

If I could change the past and live my life over, I'd do a lot of things differently. I'd be more laid-back – I'd worry less about small or imaginary problems and maybe a little more about things that really matter. I'd complain less about unimportant things. I'd slow down and take each day as it comes. I'd be more patient with people.

I'd stop being afraid of making mistakes and make an effort to try new things. I'd learn to scuba dive and speak a new language. I'd do things I enjoyed, even if I wasn't good at them, like playing the piano. I'd continue with my lessons and wouldn't give up because I wasn't all that good. I would enjoy what I could do and not worry about what I couldn't do. Yes, I'd still be competitive – I wouldn't want to change that – but I wouldn't get upset if I didn't win.

I'd try to make a difference in people's lives. I'd be more generous – with my money and especially my time. Maybe do more volunteer work. I'd spend more time listening to the stories that older people have to tell without looking at my watch and thinking about the other things I could be doing. I'd get to know my neighbors and offer to help those I knew needed help or who had problems. I would ask people on the bus, "What's wrong?" if they seemed upset.

If I could change the last few years, I'd find more time to share long and laughter-filled meals with friends or family and spend less time shut away with my computer, working. I'd be more considerate. I'd send more handwritten thank-you notes and tell people what they mean to me. I would be completely reliable, someone that everyone can count on.

If I had another chance, I wouldn't read so much about celebrities' lives. I mean, who cares? I'd spend less time in malls and more time in parks, flying a kite, or watching the birds. I'd clean the house less and read more. I'd walk barefoot on beaches and feel the sand between my toes and the sun on my face. I'd spend a summer on a Greek island, see the Pyramids in Egypt, climb a mountain in Africa, watch more sunrises and sunsets.

Life is an incredibly enjoyable trip, but it's also incredibly short. Next time around, I'd focus more on the journey and less on the destination. You'll arrive sooner than you think.

C Find these words and expressions in the blog. Choose the best meaning and circle *a*, *b*, or *c*.

1. take each day as it comes
   a. worry life is short
   b. live for the present
   c. do nothing

2. give up
   a. start
   b. stop
   c. give something to a friend

3. upset
   a. happy
   b. disorganized
   c. unhappy

4. considerate
   a. intelligent
   b. selfish
   c. kind

5. barefoot
   a. wearing leather shoes
   b. wearing no shoes
   c. quickly

About you D **Group work** Discuss these questions.

1. What have been the most important things in the writer's life?
2. What aspects of his or her life would he or she change?
3. Do you think the writer would be a better person "next time around"? How?
4. Does the writer remind you of anyone you know? Who?
5. Do you have anything in common with the writer? If so, what?

2 Speaking and writing What would you change?

About you A **If you had last year to live over again, what would you change? Think of answers to the questions, and make notes below.**

Is there . . .

- a person you'd spend more time with? _____
- something you'd spend more time doing? _____
- something you'd spend less time doing? _____
- a place you'd go more often? _____
- something you'd take more seriously? _____
- something you'd worry about less? _____
- a sport or activity you'd try? _____
- a subject you'd study? _____

B **Pair work** Take turns. Tell your partner about some things you'd change.

"I'd spend more time with my grandpa and less time on my social network."

About you C **Read the Help note, and underline the examples of *definitely* and *probably* in the article below. Then write an article about changes you would make if you could live your year over again.**

THINGS I'D CHANGE

If I had last year to live over again, I would definitely get more exercise. I definitely wouldn't watch so much TV, and I'd probably work out more at the gym. I'd try to stop eating so many snacks, but I probably would not give up ice cream because it's my favorite snack! If I got more exercise and ate less junk food, I'd lose some weight. I'd probably feel much healthier, too.

 Help note

Adverbs of certainty in affirmative and negative statements

Notice the position of the adverbs.

*I would **definitely** get more exercise.*
*I'd **probably** work out more at the gym.*

But:

*I **definitely** wouldn't watch so much TV.*
*I **probably** would not give up ice cream.*

D **Read your classmates' articles. Does anyone want to change the same things as you?**

Free talk p. 133

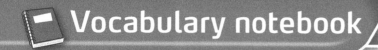

Learning tip *Verbs + prepositions*

When you learn a new verb, find out what prepositions (if any) can come after it. Remember that a verb coming after a verb + preposition has the form verb + *-ing*.

> They *apologized for* mak*ing* so much noise.

1 Read the problem below. Complete the possible solutions with the prepositions *about*, *for*, and *to*.

You forget you have a dinner date with a friend, and you don't show up.
Your friend calls you, and she is very upset. What would you do?

1. I wouldn't worry _____ it. People usually forget _____ things like that.
2. I'd apologize immediately _____ forgetting the date.
3. I'd offer to pay _____ dinner another time.
4. I'd tell her I was thinking _____ other things.
5. I wouldn't speak _____ her until she was less upset.
6. I'd blame my boss _____ keeping me in a meeting at work.
7. I'd wait _____ her to finish, and then I'd remind her _____ the time she didn't meet me.

2 Word builder Find the prepositions that go with the verbs. Then complete the sentences.

1. I agreed _____ my boss _____ the best solution.
2. He applied _____ a job with a software company.
3. I explained the problem _____ my boss.
4. I forgave my friend _____ losing my favorite sweater.
5. My neighbor invited me _____ a party last week.
6. We complained _____ the neighbors _____ the noise.
7. My parents blamed me _____ damaging their car.

On your own

Write six rules for living, using verbs that take prepositions.

My rules for living
1. Never blame other people for your problems.
2. Always forgive yourself.

Can Do! Now I can . . .

✓ I can . . .   ? I need to review how to . . .

- [ ] talk about wishes and imaginary situations.
- [ ] say how I would deal with everyday dilemmas.
- [ ] give advice with expressions like *If I were you, . . .*
- [ ] use *That would be* to comment on a suggestion or possibility.

- [ ] understand people talking about their wishes.
- [ ] understand people giving advice.
- [ ] read a blog about regrets.
- [ ] write an article about how I would change my life.

Tech savvy?

☑ Can Do! **In this unit, you learn how to . . .**

Lesson A
- Talk about problems with technology using questions within sentences

Lesson B
- Describe how things work using separable phrasal verbs like *turn on* and *plug in*
- Ask for help with technology using *how to* + verb, *where to* + verb, etc.

Lesson C
- Give different opinions with expressions like *On the other hand*
- Use *You know what I mean?* to ask someone to agree with you

Lesson D
- Read an article about email scams
- Plan and write an article about protecting personal information

1

2

3

4

How tech savvy are you? How do you use technology in your everyday life? Are you planning on buying any new electronic devices or gadgets soon?

1
Sean My computer won't turn on. Do you know what the problem is?
Mark I wonder if there's something wrong with your power cord.
Sue Mine did that, and I called tech support. But I can't remember what they said.

2
Pam There's something wrong with my tablet. It keeps freezing up. I have no idea why it's doing that.
Sally Do you know if the battery's charged?
Peter I wonder if you have a virus. Try running your antivirus software.

3
Olivia I don't know what the problem is, but I can't print anything.
Tom The last time that happened to me, I got the answer on a website. But I have no idea which site I used.

4
Cara I can't get on the Internet. Do you know what I should do?
Anita I wonder if you accidentally turned off the wireless connection. Let me see.

1 Getting started

A What kinds of problems do people have with their computers? Make a class list.

B ◀》) 3.19 Listen. What problems are the people above having? What do their friends suggest?

Figure it out **C** How do the people say the things below in one sentence? Write what they actually say. Then compare with a partner.

1. Sean What's the problem? Do you know? _____

2. Sally Is the battery charged? Do you know? _____

3. Tom Which site did I use? I have no idea. _____

4. Anita Did you accidentally turn the wireless connection off? I wonder. _____

2 Grammar Questions within sentences ◀)) 3.20

Extra practice p. 148

Direct questions	Questions within questions	Questions within statements
What's the problem?	Do you know **what the problem is**?	I don't know **what the problem is**.
Which site did you use?	Can you remember **which site you used**?	I have no idea **which site I used**.
What should we do?	Do you know **what we should do**?	I know **what we should do**.
Why is it doing that?	Do you have any idea **why it's doing that**?	I have no idea **why it's doing that**.
Is the battery charged?	Do you know **if* the battery is** charged?	I wonder **if* the battery is charged**.

Use **if for **yes-no** questions.*

Notice the word order: What **is** the problem?

Do you know what **the problem is**?

✗ Common errors

Don't use question word order for a question within a question or statement.

*I know what **you can do**.*
*Do you know what **you need to do**?*
(NOT *I know ~~what can you do.~~*
Do you know ~~what do you need to do?~~)

A Rewrite these sentences. Start with the expressions given.

1. Are there any useful new apps for students? *Do you know . . .*
   Do you know if there are any useful new apps for students?
2. What are the most popular sites for streaming movies? *I wonder . . .*
3. Which song did you last download? *Can you remember . . .*
4. Where can I get some cool accessories for a tablet? *Do you know . . .*
5. What's the most popular smartphone? *Do you know . . .*
6. How do you design your own website? *Do you have any idea . . .*
7. Will the price of tablets come down? *I wonder . . .*
8. What new technology is coming out? *Do you have any idea . . .*

About you ■ B Pair work Start conversations using the sentences above. How tech savvy are you?

A *Do you know if there are any useful new apps for students?*
B *Well, I don't know if they're new, but you can get some good grammar apps.*

3 Speaking and listening What do you know about the Internet?

**A ◀)) 3.21 Pair work Discuss the questions. Can you guess the answers?
Then listen to a conversation about the Internet. Write the answers you hear.**

1. Do you know when the public first used the World Wide Web? _____
2. Can you find out what the first webcam filmed? _____
3. Do you know what the most popular online activities are? _____
4. Can you guess how many new blogs people add to the Internet each day? _____
5. Do you know what the first email spam advertised? _____
6. Do you know what the three most common languages on the Internet are? _____

**B ◀)) 3.21 Listen again. Write one more piece of information about the answer to each question.
Then compare your answers with a partner.**

**C Pair work Student A: Read one of the answers to the questions above.
Student B: Can you remember what the question is without looking at your book? Take turns.**

((· Sounds right p. 139

1 Building language

A ◀)) **3.22** Listen. What problem is Ken having? Practice the conversation.

Ken Pedro, do you know how to get this game controller to work? I read the instructions, but I can't figure out how to do it.

Pedro Let's see. You have to turn it on first. Did you put the batteries in?

Ken Yeah. I turned the controller on — see? But the box won't work.

Pedro Oh, OK. Well, did you plug it in? Oh, yeah, you did. Oh wait, I think you need to hook up another cable. Do you know where the blue cable is?

Ken Yeah, it's here. Do you know where to plug it in?

Pedro Yes. It goes here.

Ken Thanks. Now, can you show me how to set this game up?

Pedro OK, hand me the controller. Let me show you what to do.

Figure it out **B** Circle the two correct choices in each question. Then ask and answer the questions with a partner.

1. Can you **set up a game** / **set a game up** / **a game set up**?

2. If you have a game controller, can you **hook it up** / **hook up it** / **hook the box up**?

3. If there's a problem, do you know **what you do** / **what to do** / **to do**?

4. Can you show someone **how to use** / **how you use** / **to use** a game controller?

2 Grammar Separable phrasal verbs; *how to*, etc. ◀)) **3.23**

Extra practice p. 148

Separable phrasal verbs with objects	Question word + *to* + verb
How do you ⎰ **turn on** the game controller? **turn** the game controller **on**? **turn** it **on**? (NOT **turn on it?**)	Let me show you **what to do**. Can you show me **how to turn** it **on**? Do you know **where to plug** it **in**?

A Write A's sentences in two ways using the words given. Complete B's responses.

1. A Do you know how _to turn on the TV / to turn the TV on_ ? (the TV / turn on)

   B Yeah. You need to _turn it on_ with this remote – not that one.

2. A Do you know how _____ ? (this computer / turn off)

   B Oh, you can _____ here.

3. A I can't see where _____ . (these headphones / plug in)

   B Huh. I'm not sure where _____ , either. I think they go here.

4. A I don't know how _____ on my tablet. (the volume / turn down)

   B Here. I can show you how _____ . It's easy. Look.

5. A I can't figure out how _____ . (the air conditioning / turn up)

   B I have no idea how _____ either. Oh, you need to use the remote. Here – see?

B Pair work Practice the conversations above. Practice again using different gadgets.

"Do you know how to turn on the air conditioning?"

3 Speaking naturally Linking consonants and vowels

I'm not sure how to turn it on. I don't know where to plug it in.

A 🔊 **3.24** Listen and repeat the sentences above. Notice how the consonants are linked to the vowels. Then practice Exercise 2 on page 88 again with a new partner.

B 🔊 **3.25** Listen and complete the sentences you hear. Then imagine you have a new tablet. Take turns asking and answering the questions with a partner.

1. Can you show me how to _____ ?
2. Now tell me how to _____ .
3. Can you _____ to speakers?
4. Can you show me how to _____ ?

4 Building vocabulary

A Match the pictures with the sentences. Then compare with a partner. Say what's happening in each picture.

"He's hooking up his game system to the TV."

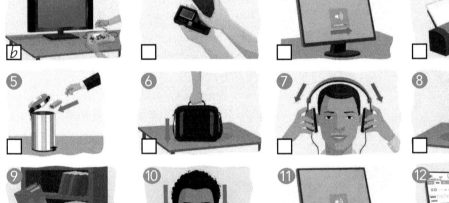

① *b* 	a. Put them away.
② 	✓ b. Hook it up.
③ 	c. Look it up.
④ 	d. Pick it up.
⑤	e. Put it down.
⑥	f. Print it out.
⑦ 	g. Put them on.
⑧	h. Take them off.
⑨	i. Take it apart.
⑩ 	j. Throw it away.
⑪	k. Turn it down.
⑫ 	l. Turn it up.

Word sort

B What can you do with the things below? Write at least two expressions from above for each item. Add ideas. Then compare with a partner.

A computer	*hook it up*	A ringtone	
A photo		A phone number	
A cell phone		Batteries	
A pair of ear buds		A printer	

About you

C Pair work Discuss the things below. Think of three . . .

Vocabulary notebook p. 94

- different things you turn on every day.
- situations when you have to turn something off.
- different things you have to plug in before using.
- things you can turn up and down.
- useful pieces of information you can look up.
- things you have thrown away recently.

A *Well, I turn my computer on every morning.*
B *Really? I leave it on all night.*

1 Conversation strategy Giving different opinions

A What kinds of online games do people play? Do you or your friends play them?

B ◀)) 3.26 Listen. What does Hugo think about playing games online? What about Greg?

Hugo	I'd get tired of playing that game by myself.
Greg	Actually, I'm playing with two other guys. See? Starship and Bronco. We play together all the time. They're kind of like friends.
Hugo	I don't know. You don't even know their real names. You know?
Greg	That's true. It's still fun, though. We're like a team. You know what I mean?
Hugo	Maybe. On the other hand, they're not *real* friends. I mean, you don't know anything about them. You know what I'm saying?
Greg	Yeah. I know what you mean, but you don't have to *know* people to enjoy doing stuff with them.
Hugo	Hmm. I'm not so sure. Don't you think it's good to spend time with real friends, face-to-face?
Greg	Sure. So why don't you come and play?

C Notice how Hugo and Greg give different opinions. They use expressions like these. Find examples in the conversation.

I know what you mean, but . . .
That's true. (You) . . . , though.
Maybe. On the other hand, . . .
I don't know. / I'm not (so) sure. Don't you think . . . ?

D Pair work Respond to each comment by giving a different opinion. Then practice with a partner. Can you continue the conversations?

1. A Playing all those online games is a waste of time.

   B Maybe. On the other hand, _____ .

2. A I spend hours on my social networking site. It's a great way to keep in touch with people.

   B I don't know. Don't you think _____ ?

3. A I never call anyone anymore; I just text. Then you don't have to make all that small talk!

   B That's true. _____ , though.

4. A I hardly ever turn my cell phone off — even at night. I hate missing calls.

   B I know what you mean, but _____ .

2 Strategy plus *You know what I mean?*

When you want someone to agree with you, you can use expressions like these.

You know what I mean?
You know?
You know what I'm saying?

It's still fun, though. We're like a team. You know what I mean?

In conversation

You know what I mean? is the most common five-word expression. It is five times more frequent than *You know what I'm saying?*

━━━━━━ *You know what I mean?*
■ *You know what I'm saying?*

Pair work Circle the best sentences to complete the comments. Then take turns saying each comment. Respond to your partner with a different opinion.

1. It seems to me that every student should have a laptop in school. **Kids need to know how to use them. / They can be distracting.** You know what I'm saying?

2. I don't think you can listen to music and study at the same time. **Music helps you concentrate. / You can't concentrate with music on.** You know?

3. They should ban cell phones from restaurants. People take business calls and everything. **It's important to be able to take business calls. / It's really annoying.** You know what I mean?

4. I guess we won't need books much in the future. Everything is online now. **We use the Internet for most things. / Books will always be more popular.** You know?

   A *It seems to me that every student should have a laptop in school. Kids need to know how to use them. You know what I'm saying?*

   B *But on the other hand, they can be distracting. You know what I mean?*

3 Listening and strategies Technology matters

A ◀)) 3.27 Listen to Karin and Sam. How would Karin answer these questions?

1. Do you know what to do when a computer freezes up?
2. What's one of the nice things about using technology?
3. How can technology help you be flexible?
4. Does it bother you if a friend you're with is always texting someone else?
5. What's one thing that annoys you about technology?

About you B ◀)) 3.28 Listen again to three of Sam's opinions. Do you agree or disagree? Write responses.

1. _____
2. _____
3. _____

About you C Pair work Discuss the questions in Exercise A above. Do you and your partner agree?

   A *Well, if my computer freezes up, I just turn it off and on again. It's easy, you know?*

   B *That's true. Most people don't know how to fix computer problems, though.*

Reading

A What is identity theft? What can happen when someone steals your identity?

B Read the magazine article. What scams does it describe? How do they work?

SAVVY AND SAFE

Most people know how to stay safe in the city: Don't walk alone after dark, hold onto your bag on crowded subways, and only ride in registered cabs. However, many people are not so savvy when it comes to staying safe on the Internet and don't know what to look for. Identity theft – when thieves steal your personal information and use your identity to open bank or credit card accounts or take out home loans in your name – is on the rise. In some cases, thieves charge thousands of dollars to credit cards, empty bank accounts, and can ruin your credit. Criminals are getting better at cheating you out of your money. What's worse is that they sometimes do it with your help. To avoid becoming a victim of an Internet scam, know what to look for.

DON'T BE THE VICTIM OF A SCAM

The friend in need scam Have you ever received an email from a friend who is overseas and urgently needs you to send money? Emma Park did, and it cost her $2,000. Emma, 22, from Chicago, was the victim of a scam. Somebody hacked into her friend's email account and sent urgent messages to everyone in the contacts list. Emma didn't even think of calling her friend to check if the email really was from him. She sent the money, and by the time she realized it was a scam, it was too late. Emma never got her money back.

DON'T send money to anyone if you get an email like this.
DO contact your friend to ask if there is a problem.

Information-request scam Your bank sends an email saying it has lost customer data. It asks you to send your bank account details, including your full password and PIN[1]. At least the email *looks* as if it's from your bank. It has their logo and looks official.

DON'T reply! Banks and credit card companies *never* ask for your full password or PIN in this way.
DO check the spelling and grammar. If there are mistakes, the email is probably a scam.

The "make money fast" chain email scam Someone sends you an email with a list of names. It asks you to send a small amount of money to the person at the top of the list, delete that name, and add your name to the bottom. The email explains that when your name gets to the top of the list, you'll receive a lot of money. You might even become a millionaire! Usually, however, the scammer's name stays at the top of the list, so he or she gets all the money.

DON'T forward the email. Sending this type of chain email is not only expensive, but it's also illegal.
DO block the sender, and block any emails that come from names you don't recognize.

Being savvy about scams is the best way to stay safe. If something seems a little strange, it probably is. Don't fall for it.

1. *PIN*: Personal Identification Number

C **Are these sentences true or false according to the article? Write *T* or *F*.**

1. Most people know how to recognize scams on the Internet. _____
2. Identity theft is increasing. _____
3. Emma lost $2,000 of her own money. _____
4. Emma sent money to a friend who was traveling overseas. _____
5. Your bank may ask you for your password if they lose it. _____
6. Your name will never get to the top of the list in the chain email. _____

About you **D** **Pair work** **Discuss the questions.**

1. Have you or people you know received emails like the ones in the article?
2. How often do you get emails from people you don't know? What do you do with them?
3. How do you keep your personal information safe online?
4. What other scams have you heard about?

2 Speaking and writing Keeping it safe

About you **A** **Group work** **Brainstorm ideas on how to keep your personal information safe. Discuss the questions and take notes.**

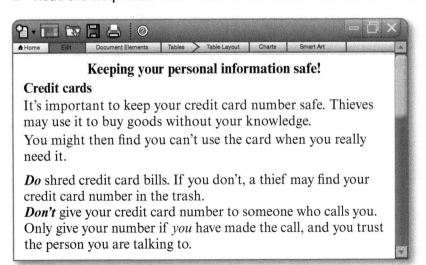

1. Which documents should you shred? Do you shred them?
2. Do you memorize your PINs? Would you ever tell anyone your PIN?
3. Where do you keep important documents? Do you have copies of them?
4. What do you have passwords for? How can you choose a good password?
5. How can you shop safely online or on the phone?
6. What can you do to protect your credit or debit card information?
7. What precautions do you take when you use an ATM?
8. How else can people keep their personal information safe?

"Well, you should shred your bank statements. I don't usually do it, though. I forget. You know?"

B **Read the Help note. Then write a short article like the one below.**

Keeping your personal information safe!

Credit cards
It's important to keep your credit card number safe. Thieves may use it to buy goods without your knowledge.
You might then find you can't use the card when you really need it.

Do shred credit card bills. If you don't, a thief may find your credit card number in the trash.
Don't give your credit card number to someone who calls you. Only give your number if *you* have made the call, and you trust the person you are talking to.

Help note

Planning your article
- Write all your ideas down in any order. Don't worry about spelling and grammar.
- Choose the best ideas you want to use.
- Number your ideas to help you plan your article.
- Write the article.
- Check your spelling and grammar.

C **Read your classmates' articles. What tips did you learn?**

 Free talk p. 134

Vocabulary notebook / On and off

In conversation

The top six things people talk about **turning on** and **turning off** are their:

1. radio   4. phone
2. light(s)   5. computer
3. music   6. television

Learning tip *Writing short conversations*

When you learn expressions with a new or complex structure, think of everyday situations where you might use them. Write short conversations using the expressions.

1 **Complete the conversations. Use the sentences in the box.**

I'll look it up.	✓ I'll turn it down. Then I'd take them off.
I'll print it out. I'll turn it up.	You can put them away in the closet.

1. A The music's too loud.   B *I'll turn it down.*

2. A I don't know what to do with these boxes.   B _____

3. A What does this word mean?   B _____

4. A I need a copy of that document.   B _____

5. A I can't hear the radio.   B _____

6. A I think I'm allergic to these earrings.   B _____

2 **Word builder Find the meaning of the phrasal verbs in the sentences below. Think of a situation for each one, and write conversations.**

1. A _____
   B Sure. What time should I **pick** you **up**?

2. A _____
   B It's a nice color. Why don't you **try** it **on**?

3. A _____
   B **Take** it **back** to the store.

4. A _____
   B Can I **call** you **back** tonight? I'm late.

5. A _____
   B OK. I'd better **take** it **out** right now.

6. A _____
   B I'll show you how to **put** it **together**.

On your own

Make labels with different expressions to put around the house. When you have learned the expression, you can throw the label away.

Take it out.

Can Do! Now I can . . .

✓ I can . . .   ? I need to review how to . . .

- [ ] talk about problems with technology.
- [ ] ask and describe how things work.
- [ ] give different opinions using expressions like *On the other hand* . . . .
- [ ] ask someone to agree with me using expressions like *You know what I mean?*

- [ ] understand a conversation about the Internet.
- [ ] understand people talking about the pros and cons of technology.
- [ ] read an article about email scams.
- [ ] plan and write an article about protecting my personal information.

1 How many words can you remember?

A How many different phrasal verbs can you use to complete the sentences below?

What can you say about relationships?		What can you do to a television?	
	get along with someone.		*turn it on.*
You can		You can	

B Pair work Compare with a partner. Score 1 point for each correct sentence. Score 2 points for a correct sentence your partner doesn't have.

2 Can you use these expressions?

Complete the conversation with the expressions in the box. Use capital letters where necessary. Then practice with a partner. There is one extra.

you might want to	✓ I know what you mean	don't you think	sort of
on the other hand	you know what I mean	I'm not so sure	though

Jan My boyfriend never picks up his phone. It drives me crazy.

Rob Oh, _I know what you mean_ . My girlfriend never answers hers either.

Jan That's annoying. If you have a phone, you should answer it. It's rude to ignore it, _____ ? Well, I think so.

Rob _____ . Sometimes it *is* rude to answer it, like if you're having dinner or something. _____ ?

Jan Yeah, but you can always pick it up and say, "Can I call you back? I'm having dinner."

Rob Maybe. _____ , sometimes people start talking anyway, and you can't get them off the phone.

Jan Oh, no. I can't believe it. He's *still* not picking up.

Rob _____ leave him a message. Then you can eat.

Jan Yeah, I could I guess. He never checks his voice mail, _____ .

3 Here's my problem. Any thoughts?

Write a piece of advice for each person below. Then role-play conversations in groups.

1. My best friend doesn't study enough because he spends too much time on the Internet.
2. I wish I could email my parents, but they don't know how to use their computer!
3. My boyfriend / girlfriend wants to settle down and start a family, but I don't want children.
4. I wish I had more money for travel. If I did, I could go to some pretty exciting places.

    A *My best friend doesn't study enough because he spends too much time on the Internet.*

    B *Well, you might want to talk to him about it.*

    C *I don't know. If I were you, I wouldn't say anything to him. But you could . . .*

4 I wish, I wish . . .

A What do these people wish for and why? Complete the sentences. Compare with a partner.

1. I wish I ___had___ (have) a car. If I ___had___ (have) a car, I _could go_ (can go) places.
2. I wish I _____ (know) how to swim. If I _____ (can swim), I _____ (be able to) go snorkeling with my friends.
3. I wish I _____ (can speak) Portuguese fluently. If I _____ (be) fluent, it _____ (be) easier to travel around Brazil.
4. I wish I _____ (have) more money. If I _____ (find) a job, I _____ (earn) more money. On the other hand, I _____ (not have) enough time to study.
5. I wish I _____ (not have to) work tonight. If I _____ (be) free, I _____ (go out) with my friends.
6. I wish I _____ (know) how to use more software programs so I _____ (can get) a better job.

B Pair work Use the ideas above to tell a partner two things you wish. Explain why.

"I wish I had a motorcycle. If I had a motorcycle, I could ride it to work."

5 I wonder . . .

A Rewrite these questions about the picture. Compare with a partner.

1. What is it?   Do you know _____ *what it is* _____ ?
2. How do you turn it on?   Can you tell me _____ ?
3. Does it still work?   I wonder _____ ?
4. How much did it cost?   Do you know _____ ?
5. How do you use it?   Can you tell me _____ ?

B Pair work Look at the picture and ask and answer your questions.

A Do you know what it is?
B Yes, it's an old record player. **OR** *I have no idea what it is.*

6 It's all relative.

A How many ways can you complete these questions? Use *who*, *that*, or *which*. Write them (in parentheses) if you can leave them out.

1. What do you do with electronic gadgets _____ don't work anymore?
2. What would you do if you got a gift _____ you didn't like?
3. What do you do when you see a word _____ you don't know?
4. What do you do with clothes _____ are out of style?
5. What would you do if you had neighbors _____ played their music too loud?

B Pair work Ask and answer the questions. Can you use phrasal verbs in your answers?

What's up?

☑ **Can Do!** In this unit, you learn how to . . .

Lesson A
- Talk about your news using the present perfect, present perfect continuous, *since*, *for*, and *in*

Lesson B
- Describe movies
- Talk about your social life using the present perfect with *already*, *still*, and *yet*

Lesson C
- Ask for a favor politely
- Use *All right*, *OK*, and *Sure* to agree to requests and *All right*, *OK*, and *So* to change topic

Lesson D
- Read a movie review
- Write a review

Have you done these things lately? What else is happening in your life these days? Have you . . .

been out with your friends?
done anything special?
had a party?
gone dancing anywhere?

eaten anywhere nice?
joined any clubs?
been to any concerts?
seen any good movies?

97

1 **Bob** So, what have you been doing since I saw you last?
Lois Working. That's pretty much it. I haven't been out in months. What about you?
Bob Same here. I've been working late every night. Uh . . . do you have time to grab a bite to eat?

2 **Maya** I haven't seen you in ages! What have you been up to?
Gail Well, you won't believe it, but I've been seeing a guy from work. We've gone out three or four times now, so I guess it's getting serious.

3 **Will** What have you been up to recently? I haven't seen you at the gym.
Diane Well, I've been going to a pottery class since September.
Will Pottery . . . really! So, what kind of things do you make?
Diane So far I've made eight vases and two bowls. Here's something I just made.

4 **Luis** Hey, good to see you. I see you're still doing karate.
Ahmad Oh, yeah.
Luis How long have you been doing that? About three years?
Ahmad Actually, for nine years now.
Luis Wow! That's impressive.

1 Getting started

A What kinds of things do people talk about when they are catching up with friends? Make a list.

B 🔊 4.01 Listen. What topics do the people above talk about? Were the topics on your list?

Figure it out **C** Circle the correct words to complete the sentences.

1. Bob has been **working** / **worked** late every night recently.
2. Ahmad has been doing karate **since** / **for** nine years.
3. Diane's been going to a pottery class **since** / **for** September.
4. Maya hasn't seen Gail **in** / **since** ages.

2 Grammar Present perfect continuous vs. present perfect 🔊 4.02

Extra practice p. 149

Use the present perfect continuous for an ongoing or repeated activity that started before now and continues into the present.	Use the present perfect to show the results of an activity or how many times it has happened.
What **have** you **been doing** lately? I**'ve been going** to a pottery class. ▶	What things **have** you **made** so far? I**'ve made** eight vases and two bowls.
Who **has** she **been seeing**? She's **been seeing** a guy from work. ▶	How many times **have** they **gone out** together? They**'ve been** out three or four times.

Since, *for*, and *in* for duration Use *since* with points in time.	I've been going to a pottery class **since** September. What have you been doing **since** I saw you last?
Use *for* and *in* with periods of time, but use *in* only in negative statements.	He's been doing karate **for** nine years. (NOT . . . ~~since nine years.~~) I haven't been out to eat **in** months.

In conversation

The present perfect is about 10 times more frequent than the present perfect continuous.

▬▬▬▬▬▬▬▬▬▬▬▬▬ present perfect
■ present perfect continuous

A Complete the conversations with the present perfect or the present perfect continuous of the verbs given. Sometimes both forms are correct. Add *for*, *since*, or *in*.

1. A ___Have___ you __been working__ (work) a lot recently? I haven't seen you ____in____ ages.

   B Actually, yeah. I _____ (not take) one day off _____ weeks. So yeah, I _____ (not go) out _____ ages. How about you? What _____ you _____ ? (do)

   A Well, I _____ (take) a weight training class at the gym _____ May.

2. A _____ you _____ (do) anything interesting lately?

   B Not really. I _____ (fill) out college applications _____ the last month.

   A Yeah? How many colleges _____ you _____ to? (apply)

   B Well, I _____ (send) three applications, but I _____ (not hear) anything.

3. A _____ you and your friends _____ (go) out a lot recently?

   B Actually, yeah. We _____ (go) to a few clubs lately. We _____ (have) fun.

4. A How long _____ you _____ (learn) English?

   B _____ I was in elementary school. I guess _____ 12 years now.

   A Wow. That's a long time. So, how long _____ you _____ (come) to this class?

   B _____ April.

About you **B** Pair work Practice the conversations above. Practice again and give your own answers.

3 Speaking naturally Reduction of *have*

What **have** you been doing for fun lately?	(What've)
How many times **have** you gone out this month?	(times've)
Where **have** you been hanging out?	(Where've)

A 🔊 4.03 Listen and repeat the questions above. Practice the reduction of *have* to *'ve*. Then ask and answer the questions. Continue your conversations.

About you **B** 🔊 4.04 Listen. Write the four questions you hear. Then ask and answer with a partner.

Lesson B / Movies

1 Building vocabulary

A What kinds of movies are these? Label the pictures with the words in the box.
Add other kinds of movies to the list. Which ones do you like? Which do you never watch?

an action movie
an animated film
a horror movie
a musical
a (romantic) comedy
a science-fiction movie
a thriller
a war movie

B 🔊 4.05 What kind of movie is each person talking about? Complete the descriptions with a type of movie. Then listen and check your answers.

1 It's a _____ . **It's about** these two people who **fall in love** over the Internet. It's a great **love story,** and it's **funny**, too.

2 It's a new _____ **set in** ancient China. Michelle Yeoh is in it. The **stunts** and the kung-fu **fight scenes** are amazing. It's kind of **violent**, though.

3 I just saw this _____ . A family moves into an old house, and they find a **monster** living in the attic. It was so **scary** that I couldn't watch most of it.

4 It's a _____ that **takes place** in Delhi. So, it's in Hindi, but it's **subtitled**. The **costumes**, the dancing, and the music are just wonderful.

5 It's a _____ . Matt Damon **plays** a spy who can't remember who he is. It was so exciting. I couldn't stand the **suspense**.

6 It's about **aliens** who come to take over the earth. It's a classic _____ . The **special effects** are incredible.

7 I saw this _____ about two soldiers who are brothers. It's a **true story** with a really **sad ending**. I cried a lot. It's a real **tearjerker**.

8 We saw this **hilarious** movie. It's one of those _____ for both kids and adults. Eddie Murphy is the voice of one of the **cartoon characters**.

Word sort **C** Make a word web about a movie. Use the words in bold. Then describe it to a partner.

It's a _____ .   It's about _____ .   _____ is in it .

It's set in _____ .   **Movie:** _____   He / She plays _____ .

It takes place in _____ .   It _____ .   I _____ .

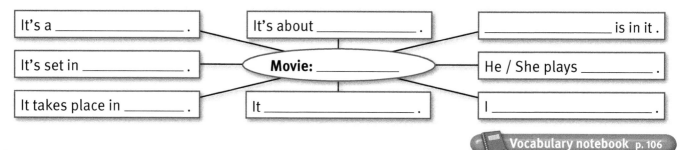

Vocabulary notebook p. 106

100

2 Building language

A 🔊 4.06 Listen. What do Carl and Jolene decide to do? Why? Practice the conversation.

Carl Sorry I'm late. Have you been waiting long?

Jolene No, just a few minutes.

Carl So, which movie do you want to see? I've heard good things about *Starship*. Have you seen it yet?

Jolene Yeah. I've already seen it. It was OK.

Carl Oh. Well, there's *Funny Guy*. It's been playing for ages, and I still haven't seen it.

Jolene Actually, I saw it when it first came out.

Carl OK, well, how about *Joker*? I haven't seen that yet, either.

Jolene I've seen it, but I'll go again. It was hilarious. At the end, the guy falls into a . . .

Carl Hey, don't spoil it for me. Let's just go see it.

Figure it out ▌ B Write the name of a movie you've seen in A's question, and circle the correct word in each response. Then work with a partner. Take turns asking your questions and giving true answers.

A I recently saw _____ . Have you seen it?

B You know, I **already** / **still** / **yet** haven't seen that movie.

C Actually, I haven't seen that movie **already** / **still** / **yet** either.

D Yeah. I've **already** / **still** / **yet** seen it.

3 Grammar *already, still,* and *yet* with present perfect 🔊 4.07

Extra practice p. 149

Have you seen *Funny Guy* **yet**?	= *I imagine you're planning to see it.*
Yes, I've **already** seen it. / Yes, I've seen it **already**.	= *I saw it earlier.*
No, I haven't seen it **yet**. / No, not **yet**.	= *I haven't seen it, but I plan to.*
No, I **still** haven't seen it.	= *I've wanted to see it for weeks, but I haven't yet.*

📰 In conversation

With this meaning of **yet**, about 83 percent of its uses are in negative statements and about 17 percent are in questions.

A Complete the conversations. Add *already, still,* or *yet.* Then practice with a partner.

1. A There's a new comedy out. Have you seen it _____ ?

   B Oh, the Ben Stiller movie? Yeah, I've _____ seen it. It was hilarious. Have *you* seen it _____ ?

   A No, I haven't, not _____ . I'd like to, though.

2. A Have you seen the latest James Bond movie _____ ?

   B No. I haven't had a chance _____ . Actually, I _____ haven't seen the last one.

3. A So, do you want to go see a movie later?

   B I don't know. I've _____ seen most of the movies that are out now.

   A Really? I _____ haven't seen any of them.

About you ▌ B Pair work Take turns asking the questions above. Give your own answers.

🔊 Sounds right p. 139

1 Conversation strategy Asking for a favor politely

A What kinds of favors might you ask a teacher for? Make a class list.

B ◀)) 4.08 Listen. What favor does Jake ask his professor? Does his professor agree?

Jake	Excuse me, Professor Carlton. I was wondering if I could ask you something.
Professor	Sure. Let me just finish up here. All right. So, what can I do for you?
Jake	Well, I wanted to ask a favor, actually.
Professor	OK.
Jake	I was wondering if you could write a reference for me. I've been applying for jobs and . . .
Professor	Sure. Do you have the information I need?
Jake	Um, yes. But not with me. Um, would it be all right if I brought it tomorrow?
Professor	All right. As long as you come late afternoon. I have classes all morning. When do you need it by?
Jake	Well, I know it's short notice, but would it be OK if I picked it up next Monday?
Professor	OK. Sure. So, was that all? All right, well, see you tomorrow!

C Notice the expressions Jake uses to ask for a favor politely. These expressions are useful in formal situations or if you are asking someone for a big favor. Find examples in the conversation.

> *I was wondering . . .*
> *I was wondering if I / you could . . .*
> *I wanted to . . .*
> *Would it be all right / OK with you if I (picked it up / came back, etc.) . . . ?*

D Complete the favors below with expressions from the box above. Then match each favor with an explanation. Write the letters *a* to *f*.

1. *I was wondering if I could* miss the next class. *d*
2. _____ get help with my homework. ____
3. _____ write me a letter of recommendation. ____
4. _____ get an extension on my paper. ____
5. _____ took some more practice tests? ____
6. _____ stayed after class to talk about my college applications? ____

a. I'm applying for a job in a hospital.
b. I need some advice about the application essays.
c. I need a little more time to complete it.
d. I have to retake a math test that day.
e. I don't understand the calculus problems.
f. I want to improve my test-taking skills.

E Pair work Take turns playing the roles of a student and a professor. Ask and respond to the favors above.

2 Strategy plus *All right, OK, So, Sure*

You can use *All right,*
OK, and *Sure* to
agree to requests.

I was wondering if I could
ask you something?

Sure.

You can use *All right,*
OK, and *So* to move a
conversation to a new
phase or topic.

All right. So, what
can I do for you?

🔊 **4.09** Listen. Write the missing words. Is the speaker agreeing to
a request (*A*), showing understanding (*U*), or moving the conversation
along (*M*)? Then practice.

> **In conversation**
>
> People also respond with just
> *Right* to show they understand
> or agree.

A I was wondering if you had a few minutes to talk.

B *Sure (A)* . Actually, I have time now before my next class. Do you want to grab a cup of coffee?

A _____ . Let's go to that place across the street.

B _____ . Let's walk over there. . . . _____ , what's up?

A Well, I wanted to ask you for a favor actually.

B Oh, _____ . _____ , what do you need?

A Well, you know I'm going away on an exchange program for two weeks.

B _____ . I heard you're going to Brazil.

A Yeah. _____ , I was wondering if you could feed my snake.

B Um, _____ . Sure.

A Thank you so much. That's great. _____ , well, can I get you a coffee?

3 Listening and strategies Favors at work

A 🔊 **4.10** Listen to four people ask their bosses for favors. Check (✓) the favors each person asks for.
There is one extra favor.

	1. Peter	2. Sandra	3. Joel	4. Julia
1. a day off work	☐	☐	☐	☐
2. to leave work early on Friday	☐	☐	☐	☐
3. more time to write a report	☐	☐	☐	☐
4. a signature on an expense form	☐	☐	☐	☐
5. to do a presentation	☐	☐	☐	☐

B 🔊 **4.10** Listen again. Why do the people need to ask the favors? Write the reason. Do their bosses
agree to the requests? Circle *Y* (Yes) or *N* (No).

1. _____ Y / N   3. _____ Y / N

2. _____ Y / N   4. _____ Y / N

About you **C** **Pair work** Take turns asking your partner for favors. Give reasons. Either agree to or decline the
favor, and say why. How many favors can you think of?

"Arturo, I was wondering if you could give me a ride home after class tomorrow?"

103

1 Reading

A Do you ever read reviews before deciding to see a movie? Are the reviews usually accurate? Tell the class.

Reading tip

Scan reviews for adjectives. They will tell you if the review is positive or negative.

B Read the movie review and the comments. What kind of movie is it? Does the review encourage you to see the movie? Why or why not?

www.avatarmoviereview...

AVATAR is magnificent, mesmerizing, and memorable!

It's an action movie, science fiction, and fantasy all in one – with, of course, some romance. *Avatar*, directed by James Cameron, is 162 minutes of thrilling entertainment. Millions of people saw the movie worldwide on its opening weekend. It went on to win **a string of** awards and **break box office records**, including the record for the **highest-grossing** film **of all time** with more than $2 billion in sales, finally ending the 12-year reign of *Titanic*.

The story takes place in 2154 on the moon Pandora, where 10-foot tall, blue-skinned, human-like creatures – the Na'vi – live in complete harmony with their environment. Pandora is rich in minerals, and humans, who have an energy crisis on Earth, have traveled to Pandora to conquer it and to mine its minerals. Since humans cannot breathe in Pandora's atmosphere, they use Na'vi-like "avatars," which they control. Sam Worthington gives an excellent performance as Jake Sully, who becomes sympathetic to the Na'vi and their desire to protect their homeland. There is inevitably **conflict** that ends **in a violent war**.

The computer-generated special effects are stunning. The music is memorable, and the invented Na'vi language is mesmerizing. All in all, it's a movie that keeps you firmly **glued to your seat**.

I have already seen *Avatar* several times now – more recently in 3D. It's one of those movies that you could watch again and again. Sad, scary, exciting – I'm sure every viewer will find his or her own way to describe the movie. If you haven't seen it yet, I recommend it. At least then you'll be ready for the **sequels**. And I, for one, can't wait.

READERS' COMMENTS:

MIKI: *I haven't seen this movie yet, and I can't comment on the acting or anything, but my friends say it's the best movie they've ever seen.*

JON: *Although it sounds good, I'm not going to see this movie. I heard it's violent in parts, and I don't like violent movies.*

SUE-ANN: *Even if you don't like sci-fi movies, you'll enjoy this one. I did!*

MARIBETH: *I loved this movie, even though I cried all the way through.*

C Find the underlined expressions in the review or in the readers' comments. Match them with the definitions. Write *a* to *f*.

1. **a string of** awards _____
2. **break** box office **records** _____
3. **highest-grossing** film **of all time** _____
4. **conflict** that ends **in violent war** _____
5. keeps you firmly **glued to your seat** _____
6. you'll be ready for the **sequels** _____

a. you won't get up, so you don't miss anything
b. a fight
c. several, one after another
d. movies that continue a story begun in a previous movie
e. do better than ever before
f. earned more than any other has ever earned

D Read the review and comments again. Answer the questions below, and then compare your answers with a partner.

1. What movie was previously the highest-grossing film of all time?
2. Why do humans need Pandora's minerals?
3. How does Jake Sully feel about the Na'vi?
4. What are two things the reviewer really likes about the movie?
5. What is one thing that might keep some people from seeing *Avatar*?
6. Will someone who doesn't like science fiction or tearjerkers enjoy *Avatar*?

2 Listening and writing   I'd really recommend it.

A 🔊 4.11 Listen to Jim and Marissa talk about a Cirque du Soleil show. Does Marissa want to see the show? Would you like to see it? Tell a partner.

B 🔊 4.11 Listen again. Are the sentences true or false? Check (✓) *T* or *F*. Correct the false sentences.

	T	F
1. Cirque du Soleil performers are all Canadian.	☐	☐
2. The group started in Quebec more than 20 years ago.	☐	☐
3. They now perform all over the world.	☐	☐
4. The acrobats perform with animals.	☐	☐
5. Jim has already seen a Cirque du Soleil show.	☐	☐
6. Jim is going to call to find out about tickets.	☐	☐

3 Writing   A Review

A Read the review and the Help note. Circle the expressions in the review that show contrasting ideas.

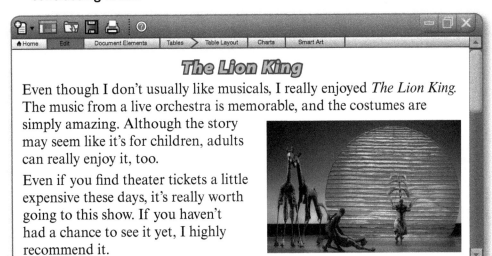

The Lion King

Even though I don't usually like musicals, I really enjoyed *The Lion King*. The music from a live orchestra is memorable, and the costumes are simply amazing. Although the story may seem like it's for children, adults can really enjoy it, too.

Even if you find theater tickets a little expensive these days, it's really worth going to this show. If you haven't had a chance to see it yet, I highly recommend it.

 Help note

Contrasting ideas

Although *the story may seem like it's for children, adults can really enjoy it, too.*

Even though *I don't usually like musicals, I loved this one.*

Even if *you don't like musicals, you might enjoy this one.*

About you **B** Think of a concert, a show, a movie, or a book you have seen or read. Write a review about it. Then read your classmates' reviews. Can you find . . .

- a concert or show you'd like to go to?
- a play you've already seen?
- a book you've been wanting to read?
- a movie you haven't seen yet?

Free talk p. 135

Vocabulary notebook / Great movies

Learning tip *Linking new words to your experiences*

When you learn a new word or expression, link it to something you have recently seen or done.

In conversation

People say *movie* 15 times more frequently than *film*.

▬▬▬▬▬ *movie*
■ *film*

1 Think of a movie title for each of these kinds of movies.

1. an animated film _____
2. a thriller _____
3. a musical _____
4. a romantic comedy _____
5. a science-fiction movie _____

6. a movie with great stunt scenes _____
7. a movie that's a true story _____
8. a movie with great special effects _____
9. a movie that's subtitled _____
10. a movie with a sad ending _____

2 Make a list of different types of movies. Link each one to a specific movie you have seen. Then write a sentence saying what the movie is about.

	Type of movie	Name of movie	What is it about?
1.			
2.			
3.			
4.			

3 **Word builder** Find out what kinds of movies these are. Put them in a chart like the one above. Can you think of the name of a movie for each one and say what it's about?

detective movie   fantasy film   historical drama   teen movie
documentary   gangster movie   martial arts movie   western

On your own

Read a review in English of a new movie. Then write a paragraph about the movie.

It's an animated film about robots. It takes place in the future. It's pretty funny.

Can Do! Now I can . . .

✔ I can . . .   ? I need to review how to . . .

☐ catch up with friends and tell them my news.
☐ say how long things have been happening.
☐ describe different kinds of movies.
☐ ask someone for a favor politely.
☐ use *All right*, *OK*, *Sure* to agree to requests.

☐ say *All right*, *OK*, and *So* to change topic.
☐ understand people asking for favors.
☐ understand people talking about going to see a show.
☐ read a movie review.
☐ write a review.

Impressions

☑ **Can Do!** In this unit, you learn how to . . .

Lesson A
- Speculate using *must, may, might, can't,* and *could*

Lesson B
- Describe situations and feelings with adjectives ending in *-ing* and *-ed*

Lesson C
- Show you understand another person's feelings or situation
- Use *you see* to explain a situation and *I see* to show you understand

Lesson D
- Read an article about *El Sistema*, a music education program
- Write an email to the founder of a charity

1

2

3

What impressions do you get from each of these pictures? Make some guesses.

What do you think is the relationship between the people in each picture?

What do you think is happening?

How do you think each person feels?

① Getting started

A Make three guesses about the picture. Who do you think the people are? How old are they? Where are they?

Emma	Hey, look. That girl over there must be graduating.
Lloyd	From college? Are you kidding? She can't be more than 12. She can't be graduating, surely?
Emma	Well, she's wearing a cap and gown.
Lloyd	Huh. She must be a genius.
Emma	Sure, but she must study a lot, too.
Lloyd	Yeah, probably all the time. She can't have too many close friends here. I mean, she's so much younger than everyone.
Emma	Well, the guy she's talking to might be one of her friends.
Lloyd	He could be. Or he may be one of her professors.
Emma	True. . . . Oh, look. Those must be her parents – the people with the cameras.
Lloyd	Yeah. They must be feeling pretty proud.

B 🔊 4.12 Listen. Emma and Lloyd are speculating about the young girl. What guesses do they make?

Figure it out **C** Complete the second sentences so they mean the same as the first sentences. Use the conversation above to help you. There may be more than one correct answer.

1. I'm sure that girl is smart. She _____ smart.

2. I'm sure she isn't older than 12. She _____ older than 12.

3. Maybe the guy she's talking to is her professor. The guy she's talking to _____ her professor.

4. I'm sure her parents are feeling proud. Her parents _____ proud.

② Speaking naturally Linking and deletion with *must*

Before a vowel sound and / h, l, r, w, y /	**Before most consonant sounds**
She must enjoy school.	*She mus(t) be a genius.*
She must have some friends who are her age.	*She mus(t) study all the time.*
She must live with her parents.	*She mus(t) feel lonely sometimes.*

A 🔊 4.13 Listen and repeat the sentences above. Practice linking the words as shown.

B Which of the speculations about the girl do you agree with? Can you add any more? Tell the class.

3 **Grammar** Modal verbs for speculating 🔊 **4.14**

Extra practice p. 150

She **must be** a genius.	=	*I bet she's a genius.*
She **must work** pretty hard.	=	*I bet she works pretty hard.*
She **must not go out** much.	=	*I bet she doesn't go out much.*
She **must be graduating** today.	=	*I bet she's graduating today.*
She **can't be** more than 12.	=	*It's not possible she's more than 12.*
He **could be** one of her friends.	=	*It's possible he's one of her friends.*
He **may be** her professor.	=	*Maybe he's her professor.*
They **might be feeling** sad.	=	*Maybe they're feeling sad.*

📱 **In conversation**

Most uses of *must* and *might* – over 90 percent – are in affirmative statements. In negative statements, people usually say *must not* and *might not* with no contractions

A Look at the pictures below. Rewrite the sentences with modal verbs. There may be more than one possible answer.

1. I'm 100 percent sure she's feeling cold.
   She must be feeling cold.

2. It's possible that she's training for a marathon.
   _____

3. I'm sure she's taking a break.
   _____

4. I'm sure she's exercising. She's not doing anything else.
   _____

5. I think she's definitely crazy to run in the snow.
   _____

6. Maybe she's trying to get in shape.
   _____

1. Maybe she's lost.
   _____

2. I bet her parents are looking for her.
   _____

3. It's possible she's in trouble.
   _____

4. I bet she's scared. It's not possible she's on her own.
   _____

5. It's possible her mother is standing nearby.
   _____

6. Maybe she's throwing a tantrum.
   _____

B **Pair work** What other guesses can you make about each picture? Discuss with a partner. Explain your guesses.

"She must be pretty tough. It looks really cold."

Building vocabulary and grammar

A ◄))) 4.15 Look at the picture. What guesses can you make about the party? Then listen. Can you identify each guest Fred describes?

Yoshi looks **bored**. **Tom** must be telling one of his **boring** stories. His stories are never **interesting**. **Sophia** seems **fascinated**, though. She must be **interested** in Tom.

Oh, no. **John** just spilled juice all over **Amy**. I bet he's **embarrassed**. She looks a bit **annoyed**. She can't be too **pleased** about her dress.

David just did something **embarrassing**. He locked his keys inside the car, and now he can't get in. That's so **frustrating**. He wanted to leave an hour ago. I bet he's **disappointed**.

What was that scream? Oh, there's a spider in **Jennifer**'s glass. She looks **shocked**. I think she's **scared** of spiders. **Ahmad** seems **surprised** by her reaction.

Andrea seems **excited** to see **Alan**. She used to go out with him. Her new boyfriend, **Albert**, must be **jealous** and a little **anxious**. He may be **worried** that she'll go back to Alan.

Word sort **B** Look at the things people say below. How are they feeling? Make guesses. Use the adjectives in bold above. Then compare with a partner.

1. "This movie's too long."
   He must be bored.
2. "I lost my house keys."
3. "Oh no! He has a girlfriend!"
4. "My vacation starts on Friday."
5. "This show is interesting."
6. "I fell and broke my glasses!"
7. "I failed the test? No!"

Vocabulary notebook p. 116

Figure it out **C** Can you complete the sentences with the adjectives given? Compare with a partner.

1. Yoshi isn't _____ in Tom's story. It's not an _____ story. (interesting, interested)
2. Sophia isn't _____ . She doesn't think Tom's story is _____ . (boring, bored)

Grammar Adjectives ending in *-ed* and *-ing* 🔊 4.16

Extra practice p. 150

Adjectives ending in *-ed* can describe how you feel about someone or something.	**Adjectives ending in *-ing* can describe someone or something.**
I'm **bored** with my job.	My job is very **boring**.
I'm **interested** in astronomy.	I think astronomy is **interesting**.
I get **annoyed** with my sister.	She does a lot of **annoying** things.
I'm **excited** about my vacation.	My vacation is going to be **exciting**.
I'm **scared** of spiders.	**But:** I think spiders are **scary**.

In conversation

Interesting, interested, amazing, scary, surprised, worried, scared, excited, exciting, and *boring* are all in the top 2,000 words.

✘ Common errors

Don't confuse *boring* and *bored*.
*I often feel **bored** at work.*
(NOT *I often feel ~~boring~~ at work.*)

A Choose the correct words to complete the sentences.

1. I get really (frustrated)/ **frustrating** when I call somewhere and they put me on hold. It's very **annoyed / annoying**.
2. We watched a really **bored / boring** TV show last night. I actually fell asleep.
3. I'm really **excited / exciting** about my trip. I'm going to Hong Kong.
4. It's really **embarrassed / embarrassing** when you forget someone's name.
5. I get really **confused / confusing** when movie plots jump around.
6. I wasn't able to get tickets to see my favorite band. I was so **disappointed / disappointing**.
7. I heard something **surprised / surprising**. Coffee might actually be good for you.
8. We went whitewater rafting recently. It was **amazed / amazing**.
9. My sister forgot my birthday. I was **shocked / shocking**.
10. We went on a huge roller coaster last weekend. It was really **scared / scary**.
11. I think documentaries about space are really **fascinated / fascinating**.
12. All of my friends think golf is **interested / interesting** to watch. I have no idea why.

About you **B** **Pair work** Make the sentences above true for you. Tell your partner.

A I get really frustrated when I don't understand something.
B Like with your homework or something? I find that frustrating, too.

3 Talk about it Feelings

Group work Discuss the questions. Write down any interesting or unusual responses, and then tell the class.

▸ Do you know anyone who is annoying? Do you get annoyed with people often?
▸ What kinds of things do you find boring? Do get bored easily?
▸ Are you scared of things like spiders? heights? flying? What's most scary?
▸ What things make you feel anxious or worried? Do you worry a lot?
▸ Have you ever felt really disappointed? What happened?
▸ Are you excited about anything right now?
▸ What's the most exciting thing you've ever done?
▸ What subjects do you find fascinating? What are you most interested in?

"One of our neighbors is really annoying.
He's always borrowing things."

🔊 Sounds right p. 139

That must be fun.

1 Conversation strategy Showing you understand

A What impressions do you get about Hal and Debra from the picture?

B 🔊 4.17 Listen. Why hasn't Hal made much progress with his saxophone?

Debra Hey, what's this saxophone doing here?

Hal I have a lesson after work.

Debra So, how long have you been playing?

Hal Oh, a couple of years.

Debra You must be getting pretty good by now.

Hal I wish! I haven't made much progress lately.

Debra Huh. How come?

Hal Well, you see, I used to practice every morning. But then I started this job, and somehow I can't get myself to practice at night.

Debra Well, you must be tired after work.

Hal Yeah. But you know, I just joined a band.

Debra That must be fun.

Hal Yeah, it really is, and it keeps me motivated to practice. In fact, that's why I joined.

Debra I see. Well, let me know if your band performs anywhere. I want to hear you play!

C Notice how Debra uses *must* to show she understands Hal's situation or feelings. Find examples in the conversation.

"That must be fun."

D Think of two responses to each sentence. Use *That must be* and *You must be* and adjectives from the box. Then practice with a partner.

1. My computer keeps crashing.
   That must be annoying. You must be frustrated.
2. I've been taking archery lessons for two years now.
3. I just got a scholarship to a master's program in business.
4. I got up at 5:00 this morning to finish some work.
5. I'm taking an ethics class. It's tough, but I'm going to finish it.
6. I'm going skydiving next week.
7. I've finished all my work, so I'm leaving early today.
8. I'm reading a long report about data security.

annoying	hard
bored	interesting
boring	irritating
difficult	motivated
excited	nervous
exciting	nice
fascinating	pleased
frustrated	scary
fun	thrilled
good	tired
happy	

About you **E Pair work** Write five true sentences like the ones above. Take turns saying your sentences and reacting to them.

2 Strategy plus *You see* and *I see*

You can use *you see* to explain something that the other person might not know.

> You see, I used to practice every morning.

You can use *I see* to show you understand something that you didn't know earlier.

In conversation

I see and *you see* are in the top 900 words and expressions.

> It keeps me motivated. In fact, that's why I joined.

> I see.

About you Complete the conversations with *you see* or *I see*. Then practice with a partner. Practice again, this time giving your own answers.

1. A Is there a country you'd really like to go to?

   B Yeah, China. _____ , my dad goes there a lot with his work, and it sounds fascinating.

   A _____ . He must have a really interesting job.

2. A Would you like to have more free time?

   B I actually have a lot of free time at the moment. I've finished my final exams, _____ .

   A _____ . You must be pleased about that.

3. A What class would you like to take if you had the chance?

   B Actually, I'd really like to learn how to blow glass. My aunt does it, _____ .

   A _____ . That must be hard to do.

3 Listening and strategies People and situations

A ◀)) 4.18 **Listen to four conversations. Match each person with the situation he or she explains.**

1. Mark _____
2. Angela _____
3. Linda _____
4. Dave _____

   a. has always dreamed of going abroad to study art.
   b. has been studying a lot recently.
   c. doesn't have enough time to practice.
   d. wants to be able to talk to people while on vacation.

B ◀)) 4.18 **Listen again. Show you understand. Write a response to each person using *must*.**

1. _____   3. _____
2. _____   4. _____

About you C Pair work Discuss the questions below.

1. What have you always dreamed of doing?   3. What don't you have enough time to do?
2. What have you not been doing a lot this year? 4. What do you want to be able to do on vacation?

   A *Well, I've always wanted to drive a race car. You see, I follow all the Formula One races.*

   B *That must be fun. Do you actually go to any of the races?*

Free talk p. 135

1 Reading

A What kinds of cultural activities are available in your area? Have you ever participated in any of them? Tell the class.

B Read the article. How does El Sistema benefit young people?

 Reading tip

Before you read a factual piece, ask yourself questions like *What is it? Where is it? Who does it?* Then scan the text to see if you can find answers.

EL SISTEMA

Venezuela has a revolutionary and inspiring music education program, which aims to improve the lives of disadvantaged children and their families. *El Sistema* – meaning "the system" – is a total-immersion[1] program that brings children together to play music every day. Preschool children sit on their mothers' knees to sing, play rhythm games, or play with paper instruments that they make themselves. At age five, children start to play a real instrument, which is a thrilling experience for them. As soon as the children are good enough, they teach the younger ones. The program is highly successful. By high school, students are tackling some of the most difficult pieces of classical music. However, the program is demanding, and participants need to be committed; they practice after school every day and on weekends.

There are now some 500 or so orchestras throughout the country, some of which perform internationally. Many of the young musicians have even become professionals. El Sistema graduates include conductors of the Venice Opera and Los Angeles Philharmonic and the Berlin Philharmonic's youngest player ever. According to British conductor Sir Simon Rattle, "There is nothing more important in the world of music than what is happening in Venezuela." These young musicians must surely be motivating role models[2] for other young people in their home country.

However, music wasn't the primary goal when the program began in 1975 with just 11 students in a garage. El Sistema's founder, José Antonio Abreu, was interested in "human development," or social action through music. Abreu's slogan, "*Tocar y Luchar*," (Play and Struggle) describes his hope that learning and playing music together helps children overcome academic, social, and economic obstacles. "If you put a violin in a child's hands, that child will never hold a gun," he is quoted as saying. Interestingly, 90 percent of the program's funding comes from social service agencies rather than cultural organizations. Since 1975, El Sistema has made an amazing difference in many lives. Two million graduates have become skilled musicians, and according to Abreu, they are resilient, flourishing citizens, as well. More than 25 countries, including the United States, Austria, and India, have since copied El Sistema's groundbreaking[3] model[4].

1 *total-immersion*: constant involvement in an activity
2 *role model*: someone that other people respect and copy
3 *groundbreaking*: completely new
4 *model*: type of program

C Read six people's comments about El Sistema. Are their impressions correct? Write *Yes* or *No*. Find evidence in the article to support your answer.

1. A program like that can't really work. I mean, they can't teach them to play advanced pieces. _____

2. The children must spend hours practicing. _____

3. Sir Simon Rattle must be really impressed with the program. _____

4. Some of the students may come from wealthy families. _____

5. They must get a lot of their money from arts and music organizations. _____

6. Programs like that can't work in other countries, though. _____

2 Listening and speaking People making a difference

A Look at the people and the organizations they are involved with. Can you guess what the organizations do?

Janine Licare

Arn Chorn-Pond

Ardena Gojani

1. **Kids Saving the Rainforest**
2. **Cambodian Living Arts**
3. **The International Book Project**

_____   _____   _____
_____   _____   _____
_____   _____   _____

B ◀)) 4.19 Listen to three conversations about the people and organizations above. Write three things each organization does. Were your guesses correct?

C ◀)) 4.19 Listen again. How does each student plan to get involved with the organization? Take notes. Tell the class which program you would choose to get involved in.

About you D **Group work** Think of a volunteer project you could start. Who would it help? What would it do? Present your program to the class. Choose two programs to support.

3 Writing My impression is . . .

A Read the two emails and the Help note. Circle the expressions in the emails that show impressions, reactions, and opinions.

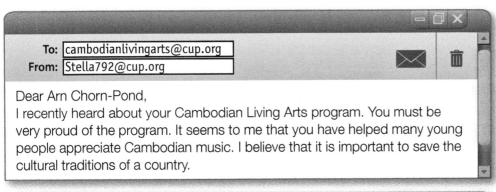

To: cambodianlivingarts@cup.org
From: Stella792@cup.org

Dear Arn Chorn-Pond,
I recently heard about your Cambodian Living Arts program. You must be very proud of the program. It seems to me that you have helped many young people appreciate Cambodian music. I believe that it is important to save the cultural traditions of a country.

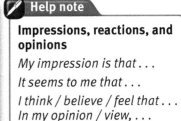

Help note

Impressions, reactions, and opinions
My impression is that . . .
It seems to me that . . .
I think / believe / feel that . . .
In my opinion / view, . . .

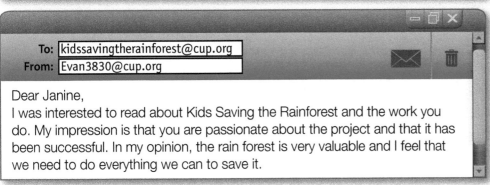

To: kidssavingtherainforest@cup.org
From: Evan3830@cup.org

Dear Janine,
I was interested to read about Kids Saving the Rainforest and the work you do. My impression is that you are passionate about the project and that it has been successful. In my opinion, the rain forest is very valuable and I feel that we need to do everything we can to save it.

About you B Which person in this lesson would you like to contact? Why? Tell a partner. Then choose one, and write an email.

C **Group work** Read your classmates' emails. Who did most people write to?

Learning tip *Linking situations and feelings*

When you learn words for feelings, link them to different situations where you might experience each one.

1 **Complete the sentences. Use the adjectives in the box or other words you know.**

annoyed   bored   disappointed   scared

1. In class, you've finished your work. There's nothing else to do. *I'd probably feel* _____ .
2. You are waiting for a friend, and she calls to say she can't meet you. *I think I'd be* _____ .
3. A friend borrowed one of your sweaters and returned it stained. *I'd feel* _____ .
4. You're on a dark street. Someone is following you. *I'd feel* _____ .

2 **Think of situations for these different emotions. Complete the sentences.**

1. I feel very motivated to practice my English when _____ .
2. I think it's annoying when _____ .
3. I was really shocked once when _____ .
4. Sometimes I get frustrated when _____ .
5. I think it's embarrassing when _____ .
6. Sometimes I get confused when _____ .

3 **Word builder** **Can you make sentences with each pair of adjectives?**

astonished / astonishing   terrified / terrifying   thrilled / thrilling   upset / upsetting

On your own

Observe the people around you during the week. Notice what they are doing, and guess how they feel. Write sentences in your notebook.

The baby's screaming. She must be hungry.

Can Do! Now I can . . .

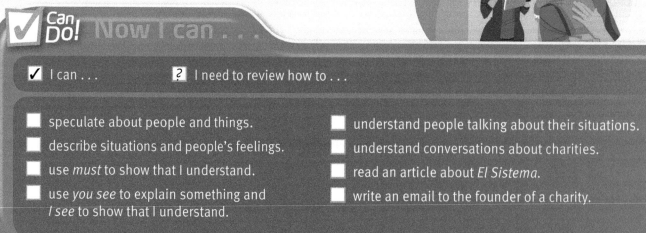

✔ I can . . .   ? I need to review how to . . .

- [ ] speculate about people and things.
- [ ] describe situations and people's feelings.
- [ ] use *must* to show that I understand.
- [ ] use *you see* to explain something and *I see* to show that I understand.

- [ ] understand people talking about their situations.
- [ ] understand conversations about charities.
- [ ] read an article about *El Sistema*.
- [ ] write an email to the founder of a charity.

In the news

✓ Can Do! In this unit, you learn how to . . .

Lesson A
- Talk about news events using the simple past passive

Lesson B
- Talk about natural disasters using the simple past passive + *by*

Lesson C
- Use expressions like *Guess what?* to tell news
- Use expressions like *The thing is . . .* to introduce ideas

Lesson D
- Read an interview with a foreign correspondent, Christiane Amanpour
- Write a survey and report statistics

How do you find out about what's going on in the world?

Which aspects of the news are you most interested in?

What major events are in the news right now?

117

Ruth   Anything interesting in the paper?

Jack   Oh, not much. Let's see. Uh, $10,000 was found in a bag on a city bus.

Ruth $10,000? I should ride the bus more often!

Jack   Yeah, and listen to this. Two large bears were seen last night in someone's yard.

Ruth   Huh. That's kind of scary.

Jack   Oh, and a jewelry store was broken into, and some diamonds were stolen. Um, what else? The city airport was closed yesterday because of strong winds.

Ruth   Really? Well, it was pretty windy.

Jack   Yeah. All the flights were delayed. Oh, and a bus was hit by a falling tree. Fortunately, the passengers weren't hurt.

Ruth   Is that all? Nothing exciting, I guess.

1 Getting started

A How often do you read local news? What local news have you read recently?

B 🔊 4.20 Listen. Jack is telling Ruth some local news. Complete the sentences.

1. Someone found _____ on a city bus.
2. There were two bears in a _____ .
3. A thief broke into a _____ .
4. The airport had to close because of _____ .
5. A falling tree hit a _____ .

Figure it out **C** Complete the second sentence so it means the same as the first. Use the conversation above to help you. What do you notice about the verbs?

1. Someone broke into a jewelry store.   A jewelry store _____ .
2. A falling tree hit a bus.   A bus _____ by a falling tree.
3. Someone saw two bears last night.   Two bears _____ last night.
4. Someone stole some diamonds.   Some diamonds _____ .
5. The accident didn't hurt the passengers.   The passengers _____ in the accident.

118

2 Grammar Simple past passive ◀)) 4.21

Extra practice p. 151

In sentences with active verbs, the subject is the "doer" and the object is the "receiver" of an action. Use active verbs to focus on the "doer" or cause.

A student **found** a bag on a bus.
The authorities **closed** the airport.
A teenager **saw** two bears in a yard.
The accident **didn't injure** the passengers.

In sentences with passive verbs, the subject is the "receiver" of the action. Use passive verbs to focus on the "receiver" or when the "doer" or cause is not known or not important.

A bag **was found** on a bus.
The airport **was closed**.
Two bears **were seen** in a yard.
The passengers **weren't injured**.

In conversation

The passive is approximately 5 times more common in written news than in conversation.

A Complete the sentences. Use the simple past passive.

1. A 500-pound bear _____ (find) asleep in a basement on Tuesday morning. The bear _____ (wake up) by a workman, who said he "freaked" when he realized it was a bear. Wildlife officers _____ (call), and the bear _____ (take) to a state park.

2. A sporting goods store _____ (break into) yesterday, and 50 bicycles _____ (steal). A white truck _____ (see) outside the store around 5:00 a.m. However, security cameras _____ (damage) during the break-in, so the thieves _____ (not catch) on camera.

3. Millions of stolen banknotes _____ (find) in a police raid this morning. Police believe the money _____ (steal) from a city bank two years ago.

4. The highway _____ (close) for several hours last night after a car _____ (hit) by an oil truck. Hundreds of gallons of oil _____ (spill) onto the highway. Two passengers in the car _____ (take) to the hospital. The driver of the truck _____ (not injure).

B Pair work Take turns retelling the stories above without looking at your books. Then prepare a story about a recent news event to tell your partner.

A *A bear was discovered in a basement last week.*
B *Right. I guess it was found after a workman went in there.*

3 Speaking naturally Breaking sentences into parts

Ten thousand dollars / was found in a bag / on a city bus.
Two large bears / were seen last night / in someone's yard.
A jewelry store / was broken into, / and some diamonds were stolen.
The city airport / was closed yesterday / because of strong winds.

A ◀)) 4.22 Listen and repeat the sentences above. Notice how long sentences are broken into shorter parts. The word with the new information in each part is stressed.

B Pair work Take turns saying the sentences above. How many times can you change the information?

"A suspicious suitcase was found in the airport terminal."

Lesson B / **Natural disasters**

1 Building vocabulary and grammar

A 🔊 **4.23** Listen. Which picture goes with each news item? Number the pictures.

1 The island of Puerto Rico was **hit** by **Hurricane** Calvin late this morning. Electric power was temporarily **disrupted** throughout the island, and many homes were **damaged** by **heavy rains** and **strong winds.**

2 Quebec was hit by **severe thunderstorms** yesterday. Flights at several airports were delayed by heavy rains, **thunder,** and **lightning.** Last night, three families were **rescued** by emergency workers after their homes were damaged by **flash floods** resulting from the rains.

3 Firefighters in Australia say over 10,000 acres of forest were completely **destroyed** by **catastrophic wildfires** this year. Investigators suspect some fires were caused by careless campers. They believe other fires started when trees were **struck** by lightning.

4 A shopping mall in Kansas was badly damaged by a **tornado** last night. A nearby town was later hit by a **freak hailstorm.** Cars were struck by **hailstones** the size of golf balls. Amazingly, no one was seriously **injured** by the tornado or the storm.

5 A small town in Italy was struck by a **minor earthquake** this morning. The quake measured 4.9 on the Richter scale. **Aftershocks** were felt in several towns. Some homes were partially destroyed, but no serious injuries were reported.

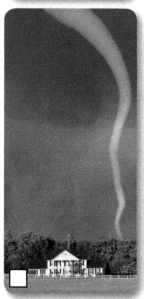

Word sort **B** Write words and expressions from the news stories in the chart below. Add your own ideas. Then compare with a partner.

Weather problems	Other natural disasters	Verbs for damage and help
hurricane typhoon	(catastrophic) wildfires	hit

Figure it out **C** Can you put these statements in the correct order?

Vocabulary notebook p. 126

1. firefighters / rescued / two families / by / were
2. was / hailstones / struck / a car / by
3. injured / was / seriously / no one
4. completely / a mall / destroyed / was / by / a fire

2 Grammar Simple past passive + *by* + agent ◀))) 4.24

Extra practice p. 151

When the "doer" of the action – the agent – is important, you can use *by* to introduce it.

Three families were rescued **by** emergency workers.
The fires were caused **by** careless campers.
A shopping mall was damaged **by** a tornado.

Adverbs with the passive

A mall was **badly** damaged.
No one was **seriously** injured.
The forest was **completely** destroyed.
Power was **temporarily** disrupted.
Homes were **partially** destroyed.

A Rewrite the extracts from news stories. Use the simple past passive with *by* + agent. Add the adverb where given in parentheses.

1. A fire destroyed an old warehouse. (partially)

   _____

2. A minor earthquake disrupted power supplies. (temporarily)

   _____

3. A hurricane damaged a high school. (badly)

   _____

4. A tornado destroyed a police station. (completely)

   _____

5. Lightning injured two golfers. (seriously)

   _____

6. Catastrophic wildfires destroyed three homes. (totally)

   _____

7. Emergency workers rescued two injured hikers in a state park. (finally)

   _____

8. High winds blew down a 500-year-old tree yesterday.

   _____

B Pair work Choose one of the news extracts above. Add details to make it into a short news report. Then read your report to the class. Which story is the most interesting?

3 Listening and speaking News update

A ◀))) 4.25 Listen to two news stories. Answer the questions.

1. What kinds of weather does the reporter talk about? _____
2. What problems did the weather cause? _____
3. Who were the people rescued by? _____
4. Why was the wedding canceled? _____
5. What happened to the groom? _____
6. What update on the story does the reporter give? _____

B Pair work Create your own news story. Role-play a TV news anchor and a reporter. Practice your story, and then act it out for the class.

Sounds right p. 139

1 Conversation strategy Telling news

A What kinds of car-related crime is there in your city? Are cars broken into or stolen?
How often do you hear car alarms?

B 🔊 4.26 Listen. What happened in Joey and Paula's neighborhood last night?

Joey	Did you hear about all the trouble here last night?
Paula	No, but I heard some police sirens.
Joey	Well, you know that older guy on the first floor of my building?
Paula	Yeah. . . .
Joey	Guess what? His car was stolen.
Paula	That's terrible.
Joey	And you know what? He heard his car alarm and called the police, but they came way too late.
Paula	I'm not surprised. The thing is, they just don't have enough police on duty at night.
Joey	Exactly.
Paula	Oh, and did I tell you? My car was broken into last Thursday night.
Joey	No. Really? Was anything stolen?
Paula	No. The only thing was, they damaged the ignition trying to start the car . . . but the funny thing was, they couldn't start it because the battery was dead!

C Notice how Joey and Paula introduce news with expressions like these. Find examples in the conversation.

Did you hear (about) . . . ?	*Guess what?*
Have you heard (about) . . . ?	*You know what?*
Did I tell you?	*You know . . . ?*

D 🔊 4.27 Listen. Write the expressions you hear. Then practice with a partner.

1. _You know what_ ? I got caught in a storm last night. My new shoes are completely ruined.
2. _____ ? The traffic is getting bad around here. We were stuck in traffic for an hour last night.
3. _____ ? They're going to open a new organic food store near here.
4. _____ ? My cousin is coming to stay with us this summer. I'm really excited about it.
5. _____ the guy I used to sit next to in class? The one with dark hair? He bought a new car.
6. _____ ? I'm getting married next spring!
7. _____ that high school principal? He crashed his car into the front of the school.
8. _____ the plans for a new skate park in the city? It's opening next spring.

About you **E Pair work** Are any of the stories above similar to stories you know? Take turns telling a partner. Can you continue the conversations?

2 Strategy plus *The . . . thing is / was*

Use *The . . . thing is / was* **to introduce ideas.**
The thing is / was . . . **(to identify a key issue)**
The other thing is / was . . . **(to add another issue)**
The only thing is / was. . . **(to raise a problem)**

Add adjectives to introduce other ideas.
The best thing is / was . . .
The funny thing is / was. . .
The scary thing is / was. . .

The thing is, they just don't have enough police on duty at night.

In conversation

Here are the most common expressions with *The . . . thing is / was*:

▄▄▄▄▄▄▄▄▄▄▄ *The thing is . . .*
▄▄▄▄▄ *The other thing is . . .*
▄▄▄ *The only thing is . . .*
▄▄▄ *The* (adjective) *thing is . . .*

A Circle the most appropriate expressions to complete the sentences. Then compare with a partner.

1. I loved everything about my vacation, but **the best thing was** / **the thing is** the food.

2. I like my college but **the other thing was** / **the only thing is**, it's too far away from everything.

3. My car was broken into once. **The funny thing was** / **The worst thing was**, they didn't take anything.

4. I was in an earthquake one time. **The worst thing was** / **The nice thing was**, I was on the twentieth floor of a building. I guess **the other thing was** / **the good thing was**, I wasn't alone.

5. My friends want me to go skiing with them this winter. **The only thing is** / **The exciting thing is**, I can't ski.

6. I get along with my brother. **The only thing is** / **The scary thing is**, he gossips too much. And I guess **the great thing is** / **the other thing is**, he's always borrowing my stuff without asking.

About you B Pair work Change the sentences above to make them true for you.

"I loved everything about my trip to Boston. The only thing was, it was very cold."

3 Listening and strategies What do they say next?

A ◀))) 4.28 Listen to four people tell some news. How do you think they started their stories? Number the sentences 1 to 4. There is one extra.

☐ You know what? There's a big hurricane coming.
☐ Did you hear the news about my sister?
☐ Have you heard about the picnic by the river next week?

☐ Guess what? The strangest thing happened last night.
☐ Did I tell you? My purse was stolen.

B ◀))) 4.28 Listen again. What comments do the speakers make? Complete the sentences.

1. The thing was, I wasn't _____ .

2. The weird thing is, _____ .

3. The thing is, _____ .

4. The funny thing was, _____ .

C ◀))) 4.29 Now listen to the complete conversations, and check your answers.

Free talk p. 136

Lesson D / **Reporting the news**

1 Reading

A What qualities do you need to be a foreign correspondent for a news organization? Make a list. Then read the interview. How many of your ideas are mentioned?

 Reading tip

After you read, ask yourself questions, for example, *What did I learn? Do I agree? What can I take away from this article?*

LIFE'S WORK:
Christiane Amanpour

An Interview with Christiane Amanpour, by Alison Beard

Christiane Amanpour gained global fame in the 1990s as a war correspondent for CNN. After a short time in the studio, she returned to foreign news reporting because "there simply aren't enough people doing it."

How did you get started in journalism?

My first job was at a local television station in Providence [Rhode Island]. They took a leap of faith with me, I think because they saw a young woman who was very serious about her career path and knew exactly what she wanted to do with her life. I was committed to journalism; I wanted to be a foreign correspondent. Today I think that's quite unusual. So I think it was the ambition I showed, the sense of mission, the desire to improve myself, and also the willingness to do anything, go anywhere.

You've said covering the war in Bosnia for CNN was a turning point in your career. Why?

That's where I really started my professional journey. I was questioned early on about my objectivity. And I was very upset about it because objectivity is our golden rule, and I take it very seriously. But I was forced to examine what objectivity actually means, and I realized it means giving all sides a fair hearing.

Has being a woman been an advantage or a disadvantage for you?

It's been nothing but an advantage. It's allowed me to get my foot into places where men have not been able to.

Your father is Persian, your mother is British, and you grew up in Iran and the UK. How did that cross-cultural experience help you in your career?

It simply made me aware, from the moment I was born, of different cultures. I've lived in a completely multicultural, multiethnic, multireligious environment, in some of the most difficult places in the world. I've seen firsthand that you can bridge differences; you can have tolerance between groups. The trick is to minimize the extremes and to stick to the sensible center.

Would you ever want to take on more of a leadership role in a news organization?

I don't know. I hope I'm fulfilling my responsibility to lead when it's necessary and to follow when it's necessary, and to encourage young people who come to me.

What advice do you give them?

Have a dream. Have a passion. Know that there's no such thing as overnight success, that success comes only with enormous hard work. And know that the only way to be good at something is to love what you do.

Source: *Harvard Business Review Magazine*

B Find these expressions in the interview. What do you think they mean? Compare with a partner.

1. take a leap of faith
2. objectivity is our golden rule
3. give all sides a fair hearing
4. see firsthand
5. bridge differences
6. overnight success

C Read the interview again. Are these sentences about Christiane Amanpour true or false? Check *T* or *F*. Correct the false sentences.

	T	F
1. She was unsure about what job she wanted to do.	☐	☐
2. She started her career in Bosnia.	☐	☐
3. She wants people to believe she is objective.	☐	☐
4. She believes that being a woman makes her job more difficult.	☐	☐
5. Her family background has helped her understand different cultures.	☐	☐
6. She believes you have to love your work to be successful.	☐	☐

2 Speaking and writing Are you up on the news?

A **Class activity** Survey your classmates, and find out their news habits. Keep a record of their answers, and then tally (卌I) the results.

News Survey

1 How often do you keep up with the news?
every day   once or twice a week   less than once a week   never

2 Where do you usually get the news?
TV   newspapers   Internet
radio   magazines   smartphone   other _____

3 What news are you most interested in?
local / regional   national   international

4 What three topics are you most interested in?
politics / current events   sports   business   science / technology
celebrities   arts / culture   the weather   other _____

B Use the information from your survey to write a report about the class's interest in the news. Use the Help note to make sure you use the correct forms of verbs.

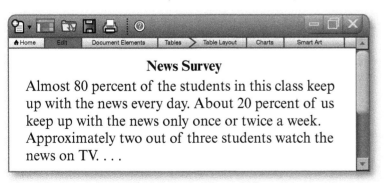

News Survey

Almost 80 percent of the students in this class keep up with the news every day. About 20 percent of us keep up with the news only once or twice a week. Approximately two out of three students watch the news on TV. . . .

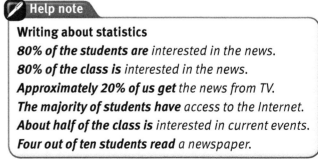

Help note

Writing about statistics
80% of the students are interested in the news.
80% of the class is interested in the news.
Approximately 20% of us get the news from TV.
The majority of students have access to the Internet.
About half of the class is interested in current events.
Four out of ten students read a newspaper.

About you **C** **Pair work** Read a partner's report. Do you agree on your findings? What information from the survey is most surprising? Why?

Vocabulary notebook / Forces of nature

Learning tip *Collocations*

When you learn a new word, use a dictionary to find out what other words are typically used with it. For example, you can say *flash floods,* but not usually *quick floods*. Or you can say *seriously injured,* but not usually *completely injured*.

In conversation

In the United States and Canada, the 6 most frequent adjectives people say before the word ***weather*** are:

1. cold   4. good
2. nice   5. warm
3. bad   6. hot

1 Look at the adjectives on the left. Circle the word that is typically used with each one.

1. **freak**   rain   hailstorm   earthquake
2. **heavy**   wildfire   tornado   rain
3. **minor**   earthquake   rain   wind
4. **flash**   tornado   earthquake   flood
5. **catastrophic**   thunder   wildfire   hailstones

2 Word builder For each sentence below, cross out the one word that *cannot* be used to complete it.

1. A building was _____ by lightning.
   a. damaged   b. destroyed   c. injured   d. struck   e. hit
2. _____ was disrupted by an ice storm yesterday.
   a. Electrical power   b. A shopping mall   c. Traffic   d. Telephone service   e. Train service
3. Two people were _____ injured.
   a. seriously   b. critically   c. severely   d. partially   e. slightly
4. The village was struck by _____ .
   a. an earthquake   b. lightning   c. a hurricane   d. hailstones   e. rain

3 Word builder Look at the expressions below. Can you figure out their meanings?

freak accident   heavy traffic   major earthquake   minor injuries

On your own

Think of three places in different parts of the world. Go online and find out what the weather is like today.

Weather Report:
Honolulu
92°F
33°C

Can Do! Now I can . . .

☑ I can . . .   ? I need to review how to . . .

- ☐ talk about news events.
- ☐ talk about natural disasters.
- ☐ use expressions like *Guess what?* to tell news.
- ☐ introduce ideas with expressions like *The thing is . . . .*
- ☐ understand news stories.
- ☐ listen to people telling personal news.
- ☐ read an interview with a journalist.
- ☐ write a report including statistics.

1 What can you guess about Suki?

A Look at the pictures of Suki's apartment. What has she been doing? What has she finished? Complete each sentence with the present perfect or present perfect continuous.

There are two pots on the stove, so she *'s been cooking* (cook). She _____ already _____ (bake) some cookies. She _____ (write) a letter, but she _____ (not finish) it yet. There's a whole pizza, so I bet she _____ (not eat) lunch. Her headphones are on the table, so she _____ probably _____ (listen) to music. Her paints and brushes are out, so it looks like she _____ (paint). She _____ already _____ (paint) a vase of flowers.

B **Pair work** Make more guesses about Suki and the pictures. Use *must*, *may*, *might*, *can't*, or *could*.

"She must like pizza." *"She might be an art teacher."*

2 That must be interesting!

Complete A's statements with *since*, *for*, or *in*, and add an adjective to B's responses. Practice with a partner. Then practice again, making the sentences true for you.

1. A I've been taking dance lessons _____ I was a kid. B You must be _____ .
2. A I haven't heard from my boyfriend _____ ages. B You must be _____ .
3. A I've been going out with someone _____ several months now. B That must be _____ .
4. A I've been working hard _____ May. I haven't had a vacation. B That must be _____ .

"I've been taking piano lessons since I was five." *"You must be really good."*

3 Have you seen any good movies lately?

Complete the chart with three movies you've seen. Discuss with a partner.

Name of movie	Type of movie	What was it like?
The Hunger Games	science fiction / drama	The suspense was unbearable.
1.		
2.		
3.		

A *Have you seen any good movies lately?*

B *Yeah. I saw The Hunger Games. It was so good!*

A *I read the book, but I haven't seen the movie yet.*

Can you complete this conversation?

Complete the conversation with the words and expressions in the box. Use capital letters where necessary.

| all right | ✓guess what | I was wondering | the only thing is | yet |
| already | I see | that must be | the thing is | you know what |

Ana _Guess what_ ? We have a new boss – Abigail Freeman. And _____ ? Things are going to change around here!

Nat Really? So, have you met her _____ ?

Ana No, but I've _____ heard lots of stories about her. _____ , she's a "clean freak." She hates clutter. So everyone is busy cleaning and putting things away.

Nat _____ . So I guess we're going to have to clean up this mailroom.

Ana Actually, _____ if we could start now because she might come by later.

Nat Yeah. We need to make a good first impression. _____ , every time I clean up, I lose something!

Ana Really? _____ frustrating! So let's be careful when we throw things away!

Nat Good idea. _____ , let's get started!

5 **I was wondering . . .**

Pair work Think of two more favors to add to the list below. Then think of a way to ask politely for each favor. Role-play conversations.

1. Ask a teacher for more time to finish an assignment.
2. Ask a friend to give you a ride to the airport.
3. _____
4. _____

A *Excuse me. I was wondering if I could have more time to finish my assignment.*
B *Well, can you tell me why you need more time?*

6 **Here's the news.**

A **Complete the news report. Use the simple past passive.**

Four cars _____ (involve) in an accident on the highway this morning. The accident _____ (cause) by a truck that spilled hundreds of tomatoes onto the road. Fortunately, the drivers _____ seriously _____ (not injure). Two people _____ (take) to the hospital with minor injuries. The truck driver _____ (interview) by police. The highway _____ (open) again two hours later.

B **Pair work** Brainstorm words and expressions describing extreme weather and natural disasters. Then write five sentences to create a news report. Read your report to the class.

| *severe thunderstorm* | *heavy rains* |

^{UNIT} **7** **Your ideal partner**

1 **Group work** What do you think people look for in an ideal life partner? Discuss the ideas below and add your own. Which of these things matter most to you?

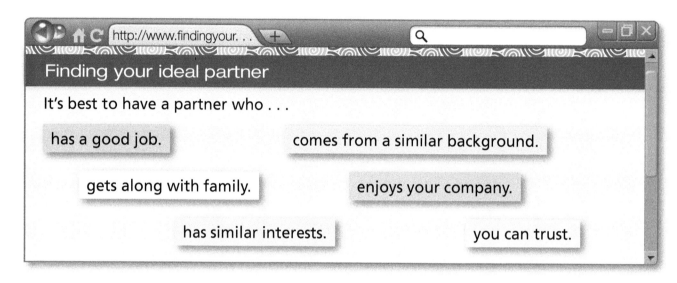

Finding your ideal partner

It's best to have a partner who . . .

has a good job.

comes from a similar background.

gets along with family.

enjoys your company.

has similar interests.

you can trust.

A *I guess it's good to choose someone who has a good job.*

B *Well, you probably don't want a partner who's only interested in work, though.*

2 **Group work** What ten questions should people always ask their partner before they decide to get married? Discuss your ideas and give reasons. Decide on the ten most important questions.

"You should ask, 'How many times have you broken up with someone?'"

UNIT 8 **What would you do?**

Group work Discuss the questions. How are you alike? How are you different?

1. If you had an hour to spare right now, what would you do?

2. If you had one month of free time, what would you do?

3. If you had to choose one thing to keep throughout your life, what would it be?

4. If you had to choose one electronic gadget to live without, what would it be?

5. If you could invite a famous person to a party, who would you invite?

6. If you could be like one person, who would you want to be like?

7. If you could have any job, what kind of work would you do?

8. If you could have one special talent, what would it be?

9. If you had to give up one habit, what would it be?

10. If you could do one thing over, what would you do?

A *If you had an hour to spare right now, what would you do?*
B *I'd play computer games!*
C *Really? I wouldn't. I'd go and hang out with my friends.*

Technology etiquette

Pair work Read the opposite opinions in the chart below. Debate each pair of arguments.
Do you agree?

1.

It's perfectly fine to have a long conversation on your phone when you're out with a friend.

OR

You should turn your phone to vibrate when you're out with friends and only take urgent calls.

2.

It's OK to play loud music on a beach or in a public place.

OR

You should always listen to your music with your headphones on.

3.

You don't need to return voice-mail or text messages right away.

OR

It's important to return a message immediately.

4.

Microblogging is fun. It's a great way to keep up with what's going on with your friends.

OR

Microblogging is a complete waste of time. Who wants to know all those silly details about people's lives?

5.

It's OK to "unfriend" people on your social networking site and not tell them.

OR

You shouldn't unfriend people – it can hurt their feelings.

6.

It's OK to post photos of your friends online.

OR

You shouldn't do that. You should always ask permission first.

A *Well, I don't see why you should turn your phone off or put it onto vibrate when you're out with friends. I don't really see what the problem is with taking calls. You know?*

B *I know what you mean. But it can be annoying when you're trying to have a conversation with someone and their phone keeps ringing.*

UNIT **10** **Who's been doing what?**

Class activity Find classmates who answer yes to the questions. Write their names in the chart. Write notes about each person. Tell the class two interesting things you learned.

Find someone who's been . . .	Name	Notes
planning something special.	_Ana_	_has been planning a birthday party_
helping a friend with something.		
working or studying too much lately.		
taking a fun class or learning something new.		
going to the movies a lot.		
hanging out with their friends a lot.		
watching a series on TV.		
thinking about taking a trip.		
trying to give up a bad habit.		
eating out a lot.		

A *Ana, have you been planning anything special?*

B *Actually, yeah, I have. I've been planning a birthday party for my sister.*
   OR   *No, I haven't. I haven't planned anything special for ages.*

UNIT **11** **That must be fun!**

1 Write true sentences for each conversation below. Make sure your sentences make sense with the responses given.

1. **You** _____ B That must be fun.	2. **You** _____ B You must be excited.	3. **You** _____ B That must be interesting.
4. **You** _____ B That must be annoying.	5. **You** _____ B You must be nervous.	6. **You** _____ B That must be scary.

2 Pair work Take turns sharing your sentences. Continue conversations with your classmates. Ask questions and speculate about the things they say.

A *I just started working at a museum. I'm helping them set up some displays.*

B *Wow, that must be fun. You must like your job.*

Free talk

UNIT
12 Here's the news!

1 **Pair work** Make up a short TV news report about each picture. Think of three facts for each story.

2 **Group work** Join another pair. Take turns telling your news stories.

Sounds right

◀)) 4.36 Listen and repeat the words. Notice the underlined sounds. Which sound in each group is different? Circle the odd one out.

1. <u>h</u>ot   <u>h</u>ung   w<u>h</u>ich   w<u>h</u>o

2. ano<u>th</u>er   <u>th</u>at   <u>th</u>ere   <u>th</u>rough

3. <u>o</u>ne   w<u>e</u>nt   w<u>o</u>rk   <u>wr</u>ote

4. alo<u>ng</u>   goi<u>ng</u>   si<u>gn</u>   weddi<u>ng</u>

5. play<u>s</u>   sit<u>s</u>   there'<u>s</u>   turn<u>s</u>

6. a<u>c</u>ross   <u>c</u>ircle   <u>c</u>ollege   ro<u>ck</u>

◀)) 4.37 Listen and repeat the pairs of words. Notice the underlined sounds. Are the sounds the same (S) or different (D)? Write S or D.

1. pla<u>ce</u> / ex<u>c</u>iting _S_

2. b<u>o</u>rrow / w<u>o</u>rk ____

3. en<u>g</u>ineering / for<u>g</u>et ____

4. E<u>gy</u>pt / apolo<u>g</u>ize ____

5. c<u>ou</u>ld / w<u>ou</u>ld ____

6. sh<u>are</u> / anywh<u>ere</u> ____

7. eno<u>ugh</u> / a<u>ff</u>ord ____

8. bu<u>s</u>y / choo<u>se</u> ____

9. i<u>f</u> / o<u>f</u> ____

UNIT **9** ◀)) **4.38** Listen and repeat the words. Notice that one or more syllables in each word are unstressed. They have a weak vowel sound like the /ə/ sound in *around* or the /ər/ sound in *battery*. Circle the unstressed syllables.

1. (a)round   3. computer   5. remember   7. problem   9. support

2. batt(er)y   4. idea   6. controller   8. tablet   10. virus

UNIT **10** ◀)) **4.39** Listen and repeat the words. Notice the underlined sounds. Are the sounds like the sounds in *again*, *bought*, *eat*, *made*, *there*, or *true*? Write the words from the list in the correct columns below.

1. alien   5. hilarious   9. scene

2. cartoon   6. place   10. seen

3. costume   7. saw   11. serious

4. fall   8. scary   12. suspense

again	bought	eat	made	there	true
			alien		

UNIT **11** ◀)) **4.40** Listen and repeat the adjectives. Do the *-ed* endings sound like /t/, /d/, or /ɪd/? Write *t*, *d*, or *ɪd*.

1. annoyed __d__   5. excited _____   9. scared _____

2. bored _____   6. fascinated _____   10. shocked _____

3. disappointed _____   7. interested _____   11. surprised _____

4. embarrassed _____   8. pleased _____   12. worried _____

UNIT **12** ◀)) **4.41** Listen and repeat the words. Match the words with the same underlined sounds.

1. bus __c__   a. amazingly

2. closed _____   b. catastrophic

3. flash _____   c. city

4. fortunately _____   d. damage

5. injure _____   e. much

6. shock _____   f. partially

Extra practice

7 Lesson A Relative clauses

A Complete the questions about your circle of friends. Use *who*, *that*, or a preposition, or write a dash (–) if no word is needed. Sometimes more than one answer is possible.

> **i Note**
>
> Some relative clauses end with a **preposition**.
>
> *Yuya is a guy that Jen introduced me to.* (= Jen introduced me **to Yuya**.)
>
> *Mike is the guy I run with.* (= I run **with Mike**.)
>
> *Charlie is someone I grew up with.* (= I grew up **with Charlie**.)

Who's . . .

1. a friend ___that___ you often go out ___with___ ?
2. the person in your family _____ you most often talk _____ ?
3. the classmate _____ is always interrupting other people _____ ?
4. the friend _____ you like to spend time _____ ?
5. a friend _____ you went to elementary school _____ ?
6. the co-worker _____ has the most impeccable taste in clothes _____ ?
7. the friend _____ has the best sense of humor _____ ?
8. someone _____ always makes a good impression on people?
9. a friend with a car _____ you'd like to own _____ ?
10. the friend _____ you can always rely _____ when you have problems?
11. a person _____ you sometimes have arguments _____ ?
12. the co-worker _____ you're always apologizing _____ ?

> **✗ Common errors**
>
> Don't leave out *who*, *that*, or *which* in a subject relative clause.
>
> *She works for a company* ***that / which*** *makes computers.* (NOT ~~She works for a company makes computers.~~)

About you ■ B Pair work Ask and answer the questions above.

7 Lesson B Phrasal verbs

A Complete the questions with the correct particle.

1. Did you have any friends who had to move ___away___ when you were young?
2. Did you hang _____ with a big crowd when you were growing _____ ?
3. Have you ever gone _____ to your elementary school to visit?
4. Can you think of someone who you get _____ with but don't see often enough?
5. Have any of your friends ever had a relationship that didn't work _____ ?
6. What's the most recent class you signed _____ for?
7. Why would you come _____ early from a vacation?
8. Can you think of a situation that started _____ badly but turned _____ well?
9. Have any of your friends gotten married and settled _____ ?
10. How long should you go _____ with someone before you introduce him or her to your parents?

About you ■ B Pair work Ask and answer the questions above. Give as much information as you can.

"I had one friend who had to move away. Her dad got a job in another city."

UNIT **8** **Lesson A** Wishes and imaginary situations or events

A Use the information to complete the sentences about people's behavior.

1. I'm so disorganized. I lose things all the time.
    I wish *I were less disorganized* .
    If I *were less disorganized, I wouldn't lose things all the time* .

2. My sister never pays attention in school. She doesn't get good grades.
    I wish _____ .
    If she _____ .

3. I can't take a vacation this year. I feel so stressed all the time.
    I wish _____ .
    If I _____ .

4. My parents never let me use their car. They have to drive me everywhere.
    I wish _____ .
    If my parents _____ .

5. My brother never helps clean up the house. I don't have time to do other things.
    I wish _____ .
    If he _____ .

About you **B Pair work Do you have similar wishes? Make the wishes true for you. Tell a partner.**

UNIT **8** **Lesson B** Asking about imaginary situations or events

> **✗ Common error**
>
> Use *would* when asking about imaginary situations.
>
> *What **would** you do if you missed an appointment?* (NOT *What ~~will you do~~ if you missed an appointment?*)

A Make questions about these imaginary situations using the words given.

1. A friend talks about you behind your back. / You say something.
    What would you do if a friend talked about you behind your back
    (what / you / do)? Would you *say something* ?

2. You forget an important homework assignment. / You give your teacher an excuse.
    _____ (how / you react)? Would you _____ ?

3. You don't meet a big deadline. / You apologize to your boss.
    _____ (what / you / do)? Would you _____ ?

4. Your parents buy you a present that you don't like. / You tell them the truth.
    _____ (what / you / say)? Would you _____ ?

5. A friend invites you to a party that you don't want to go to. / You say you're busy.
    _____ (how / you / react)? Would you _____ ?

6. You lend some money to a friend, and she forgets about it. / You remind her about it.
    _____ (what / you / do)? Would you _____ ?

About you **B Pair work Ask and answer the questions above. Add other reactions and solutions to the problems.**

"What would you do if a friend talked about you behind your back? Would you be very upset?"

Lesson A Questions within sentences

A Unscramble the questions, and complete the answers with your own information.

1. you know / has / your computer / do / how much memory

    Q: _Do you know how much memory your computer has_ _____?

    A: No, actually, I can't remember _____.

2. how many hours / do / you / online each week / spend / you have any idea

    Q: _____?

    A: A lot! I don't know exactly _____.

3. you know / do / is / a good wireless Internet connection in your classroom / there / if

    Q: _____?

    A: Well, I don't know _____.

4. every week / you know / do / how many text messages / you / send

    Q: _____?

    A: Not really. I don't really know _____.

5. you remember / sent / can / who / you / emails to yesterday

    Q: _____?

    A: Yes, I can remember exactly _____.

About you B Pair work Ask and answer the questions. Give your own answers.

Lesson B Separable phrasal verbs; *how to, where to, what to*

> **✗ Common errors**
>
> Don't put object pronouns like *it*, *them*, etc. after the particle (*on*, *up*, etc.).
>
> *Can you **turn it off**?*
> (NOT *Can you ~~turn off it~~?*)

A Complete the first questions using the words given. There are two correct answers. Then complete the second questions using pronouns.

1. How often do you __turn off your cell phone__ OR
    __turn your cell phone off__? (your cell phone / turn off)
    When do you have to __turn it off__?

2. Did you know how to _____? (your computer / set up)
    Did you _____ yourself?

3. Has anyone ever asked you _____? (your music / turn down)
    Did you _____?

4. Do you _____ to listen to music? (your headphones / put on)
    Did you _____ yesterday?

5. Do you know how to _____ on your computer? (the spell check / turn on)
    Do you usually _____?

6. Do you know how to _____ in your home? (wireless Internet / set up)
    Did you _____?

About you B Pair work Ask and answer the questions with a partner. Give your own answers.

UNIT 10 Lesson A Present perfect continuous

A Complete the questions with the verbs given. Use the present perfect continuous.

1. _____ you and your friends _____ (eat out) a lot recently?
2. What _____ you _____ (do) today? _____ you _____ (do) anything interesting?
3. How long _____ you _____ (work) in your current job?
4. _____ you _____ (go out) a lot during the week?
5. How long _____ you and your friends _____ (hang out) together?
6. _____ your best friend _____ (take) other classes this year?
7. _____ you _____ (follow) any sports teams this year?
8. How long _____ you and your family _____ (live) in your apartment or house?
9. How long _____ your best friend _____ (learn) English?
10. How long _____ you _____ (study) today? _____ you _____ (study) all day?

About you **B** Write your own true answers to the questions above. Write at least one sentence using the present perfect continuous, and one sentence using the present perfect.

1. Actually, we've been eating out every Friday. We've been to a couple of nice restaurants.

About you **C** Pair work Ask and answer the questions above. Ask follow-up questions for more information.

> ✖ **Common errors**
>
> Don't use the present with *for* or *since* to talk about past time.
>
> ***I've been taking** this class for nine months, since September.* (NOT *~~I'm taking~~ this class . . .*)

UNIT 10 Lesson B *already*, *still*, and *yet* with present perfect

A Write the title of a TV show, two movies, a book, a singer, and a place in the conversations. Then complete the conversations with *already*, *yet*, or *still*.

1. A You know, there's a new show on TV – _____ . I haven't seen it _____ . Have you?
   B No. I've heard about it, but I haven't seen it _____ , either. It looks good.

2. A You know that new movie, _____ ? Have you seen it _____ ?
   B Yes, I've _____ seen it. It was good. But I _____ haven't seen _____ . I'd like to see that, too. Actually, there are a few movies that I _____ want to see.

3. A Have you read any good books recently? I just read _____ . Have you read it?
   B No, I haven't read it _____ . I've been busy. I _____ haven't read the book assignment for my English class.

4. A Have you heard _____ 's new song _____ ?
   B No. I haven't downloaded it _____ . I _____ haven't heard the other songs on the album, either.

5. A There are a lot of great places to visit in the city, but I've never been to _____ . Have you?
   B No, I haven't been there _____ . I _____ haven't been to some of the museums or art galleries either.

About you **B** Pair work Practice the conversations above. Then practice again, giving your own answers.

Extra practice

Lesson A Modal verbs for speculating

> **✕ Common errors**
>
> Don't use *can* to speculate.
>
> *It's snowing, and she's not wearing a coat. She must be cold.*
> (NOT *She can be cold.*)

A Make guesses about the situations below. Complete the sentences with modal verbs and the verbs given. Sometimes there is more than one correct answer.

1. You hear the sound of breaking glass at your neighbor's house next door, and then a siren.
   a. It _must be_ (be) a burglar for sure.
   b. The neighbors _____ (be) away, perhaps.
   c. The police _____ (come).
   d. The burglar _____ (be) in the house.

2. You see a young woman and young man talking outside a cinema. They look upset.
   a. They _____ (have) an argument.
   b. They _____ (feel) very happy.
   c. He _____ (be) her date, perhaps.
   d. He _____ (try) to comfort her.

3. You're in a cab that is going too fast.
   a. The driver _____ (be) in a hurry, for sure.
   b. He _____ (be) a very safe driver.
   c. He _____ (break) the speed limit.
   d. He _____ (want) to get off work early.

4. You see a cyclist sitting on the ground next to his bike.
   a. He _____ (be) hurt, perhaps.
   b. He _____ (take) a rest.
   c. He _____ (take part) in a bicycle race.
   d. His bicycle _____ (be) damaged.

B Pair work What other guesses can you make about each situation? Discuss with a partner. Explain your guesses.

Lesson B Adjectives ending in *-ed* and *-ing*

A Complete the sentences. Write the correct adjective forms of the words given.

1. I hate it when I'm out with a group of friends and we can't decide what to do. It can be incredibly _____ (frustrate). I guess we're all _____ (interest) in different things.
2. I get really _____ (annoy) when people say they'll meet me and then they're half an hour late. It's _____ (surprise) how selfish people can be.
3. My parents are very _____ (please) that I have nice friends. I think parents get _____ (worry) about things like that.
4. I'm always really _____ (shock) when friends get into fights with each other.
5. It's always _____ (excite) to see my friends. Not one of them is _____ (bore).
6. It's _____ (disappoint) when friends don't keep in touch. But it happens.
7. I feel _____ (disappoint) when friends don't call when they promised.
8. Some people post really mean comments online. They can be pretty _____ (scare).
9. It's always _____ (fascinate) to find out about other people's jobs.

About you **B** Pair work Discuss the sentences above. Do you agree?

"It's very frustrating when I'm out with friends and we can't decide what to do. I think we all just have a hard time choosing something interesting."

UNIT **12** **Lesson A** Simple past passive

A Write sentences using the prompts given and the simple past passive.

1. A dinosaur bone / find / in a storage box at a Boston museum this week.

   _____

   The bone / identify / as a new species of dinosaur.

   _____

2. Two main subway lines / close / yesterday for a second day.

   _____

   Repairs to the lines / not complete / on time.

   _____

3. A live show in New York City / cancel / last night after the lead singer fell off the stage.

   _____

   Ticket holders / not refund.

   _____

4. Police / call / to an apartment after neighbors heard strange sounds.

   _____

   A raccoon / trap / inside the apartment. It / remove / by animal services.

   _____

About
you **B** **Pair work** How many more ideas can you add to the news reports above? Take turns making suggestions.

"The dinosaur bone was found by a student who was working at the museum."

UNIT **12** **Lesson B** Simple past passive + *by* + agent

A Rewrite the two news stories using the prompts given. Use the simple past passive and an adverb. Use *by* where needed.

1. A thief broke in through the roof of a police station late last night – thinking it was a local business. The roof (partial / damage) when the thief fell through and landed on the floor of the police station. The man (quick / arrest / an officer on duty). Although the man (serious / not injure), he (immediate / take to the emergency room / ambulance). Police say the burglar alarms at the station (temporary / disconnect).

   _____
   _____
   _____

2. Dozens of cars (bad / damage) yesterday after a freak hailstorm. The cars (hit / large hailstones) in the parking lot of a local supermarket. One driver said her windshield (complete / shatter). The store (partial / flood) in the storm.

   _____
   _____
   _____

B **Pair work** Take turns retelling the two news stories without looking at your books.

Illustration credits

Photography credits

Text credits

Answers

Unit 3, Lesson A

1 Getting started, Exercise B, page 22

1. b Taipei. Taipei 101 is the tallest office building in the world.
2. a Japan. The Akashi-Kaikyo Bridge is the longest suspension bridge.
3. b China. The New South China Mall is the largest shopping mall.
4. b Moscow. McDonald's is the world's busiest restaurant.
5. c Barcelona. Camp Nou is the largest soccer stadium in Europe.
6. c France.

1 Getting started, Exercise C, page 22

1. What's the <u>biggest</u> train station in the world?
   Grand Central Station in New York City. It has the most platforms.
2. What's the <u>busiest</u> airport in the world?
   Harsfield-Jackson Atlanta International Airport in Georgia, U.S.A. It has the most passengers.
3. Where is the <u>largest</u> building in the world?
   Boeing Everett Factory in Washington, U.S.A. It has the most usable space.
4. What's the <u>most expensive</u> city in the world?
   Tokyo.